ALAN RUTKOWSKI

How to Avoid Grammar Gaffes Once and for All

Second Canadian Edition

ICELARK MEDIA INC.

National Library of Canada Cataloguing in Publication

ISBN 978-0-9693658-8-4

Alan Rutkowski/Rutkowski Alan
How to Avoid Grammar Gaffes Once and for All
Second Canadian Edition

English Language Grammar—English Language Style—English Language Vocabulary—English Language Reference—English Language Usage—English Language Problems—English Language Punctuation

First published by *The Edmonton Journal* in 2007 as "Grammar Gaffes."

Icelark Media Inc.
info@icelarkmedia.com

I dedicate this book to my wife, Rendene,
whose many years of experience as an ESL teacher have made
her advice regarding grammatical explanations invaluable.

Alan Rutkowski

This book brings together newspaper columns that were written over a period of three and a half years. I hope readers of the book find the inevitable repetition as reinforcing as readers of the column did.

CONTENTS

FOREWORD

In 1983, Gary Larson published his memorable Dali-indebted cartoon entitled "Boneless Chicken Ranch." I think of it whenever reading prose the author of which either never received instruction in English grammar, punctuation, and style or failed to retain and use what was taught. Incorrect or inelegant prose resembles a boneless chicken: it lacks a skeleton on which all significance, identity, and character depend. We can split hairs over rules of grammar that make no difference to meaning or that affect only the tone of prose, but we cannot do without grammar's elementary rules, which somehow continue to be respected in written if not spoken English.

For someone who spends a good deal of his time at work reading and grading essays, theses, articles, and books, I encountered with pleasant surprise Alan Rutkowski's weekly column when it began appearing in the *Edmonton Journal.* During that time, he buoyed the spirits of those who think that correct prose still matters, and that fragments scrawled in the margins of memos, thumbed Blackberry notes, or blogspew just don't cut it. Moreover, those columns' quizzes have left few of its readers with a perfect score. Having grown up at a time when "I feel badly" and "just between you and I" flourished like dandelions on a suburban lawn, I was served more than a few columns' worth of humble pie, for all intensive purposes, as they say.

No martinet, Rutkowski possesses an engaging tone that encourages rather than hectors. Leaving reader unintimidated by his subject, he discusses the foibles of errors and of evolving grammatical practices in fresh ways, far better than most reference works or websites to which curiosity or embarrassment might prompt one to resort. Alan's cast of characters (Jadwiga's my favourite) is an added bonus.

Like people, a canary's food must be thoroughly cleaned before being consumed.

Explaining why such a sentence conveys a different meaning than its author presumably intended takes skill that few of us possess. Some could mark it wrong, but explaining in clear, memorable fashion why possessives matter and why comparisons require parallel structures is a talent that we do well to acknowledge in those who have it. If, like me, you were taken hostage by Whole Language Learning through the course of your education, you will appreciate those who stayed the course, raising whole chickens rather than the boneless variety, for all intensive purposes, as the egg-corners among us like to say. You might appreciate a correctly used semicolon or a correctly formed parallelism. You might find yourself arguing, perhaps even stridently, that the content of prose can only ever be as impressive as its presentation. But, as well, you might find yourself in line for a dose of correction when types like Rutkowski lead you gently to the discovery that rules (for example: Don't begin a sentence with a coordinate conjunction) by which you abided for years were made up by your teacher and aren't universally upheld—the sort of discovery up with which it's difficult to put.

No less than the first, the second edition of this book will make its mark among readers, especially those who prefer Horace to Juvenal, Chekhov to Tolstoy, Munro to Davies, being shown to being told.

As it was for the first edition, it's an honour to participate in a small way in this collection, which I know will provide instruction, verification, correction, and not a little delight.

Professor I. S. MacLaren
University of Alberta

INTRODUCTION

Linguists—not polyglots who speak many languages, but scholars who study language—are concerned with describing how a language works. That's *descriptive* grammar. English instructors are concerned with *prescriptive* grammar, that is, with teaching the grammar and usage rules of standard English. But who made the rules? In fighting what sometimes seems to us a rear-guard action against proliferating grammar errors and convoluted sentences, we can forget that grammar does not consist of immutable laws handed down by some grammar deity.

A living language spoken by sentient beings evolves and changes over time. Most of us know that a double negative is an error in standard English, but in Chaucer's time, double and even triple negatives were standard. A widespread error that I have mentioned many times is "between you and I." This usage violates the rule that pronouns must be in the objective case when they are the objects of prepositions, so the correct phrase is "between you and me." Many grammarians assume that the error arises from hypercorrection. As children, every time we said something like "Jimmy and me want to go out and play," we were corrected: "No, dear, Jimmy and *I* want to go out and play." As a result, any time some speakers combine any word with the first person personal pronoun, they make the pronoun *I* even when it should be *me*. But Shakespeare used "between you and I" in *The Merchant of Venice*, and I have read that it was a common usage in Elizabethan English. It is still considered wrong today by most grammarians, but who knows about tomorrow? If an "error" becomes widespread enough, it will eventually be considered acceptable.

Some say that correct usage is determined by what the majority of educated speakers say. But how do we determine what the majority say? Sometimes it's easy. Few educated English speakers ever say "She don't" instead of "she doesn't" (linguists would point out that in some dialects of English, "she don't" is standard.) *The American Heritage Dictionary of the English Language* uses a panel of experts to rule on controversial usages, and the rulings are never unanimous. Take the use of *impact* as a verb, for example. Ninety-five percent of the panel "disapproves of the use of *impact* as a transitive verb in the sentence *Companies have used disposable techniques that have a potential for impacting our health.*" But the usage note points out that *impact* has been used as a verb since 1601 and in its modern sense of "to affect" since 1935. (I still object to the use of *impact* as a verb for the reason the usage note suggests: it usually appears in a context of horrible jargon and inflated gobbledygook.)

Some object to making verbs out of nouns altogether, but it is a natural process in English. The word *contact* started out as a noun, but who now objects to "I'll contact you tomorrow"? In 1969, only 34 percent of the panel approved the use of *contact* as a verb; today 65 percent accept it.

Over time the meanings of words can change. Traditionally, the verb *comprise* is not interchangeable with the verb *compose.* The whole *comprises* the parts: *Canada comprises ten provinces.* The parts *compose* the whole: *Ten provinces compose* (or *make up) Canada.* Today many good and respectable writers use *comprise* in place of *compose*, especially in the passive: *Canada is comprised of ten provinces.*

Nonetheless, those of us who prescribe correct grammar and usage can take comfort in knowing that our advice is infinitely more reliable than advice on nutrition. No grammatical usage has ever changed as rapidly as the respective health benefits of butter and margarine.

Alan Rutkowski

GRAMMAR RULES

Grammar Myths

Nobody likes the grammar police. There's a joke about two women sitting on a plane. One of them, a Texan, turns to the other and asks, "Where are you all from?" The woman looks at her and answers disdainfully, "I'm from a place where people don't end sentences with prepositions." The Texan smiles and says, "Oh. Well then, where are you all from, witch?" Who doesn't side with the Texan?

English teachers are concerned with the rules of formal, written English, which few of us follow all the time. For example, in formal English only a subject pronoun (*I, he, she, we, they*) can follow any form of the verb to be (*am, is, are, was, were, etc.*). If I knock on the door and hear my wife ask, "Who's there?" I answer, "It's me." If I answered, "It is I," my wife probably wouldn't open the door.

Don't believe everything you were taught in school.

The following page contains three common grammar myths:

1. You must never split an infinitive. The infinitive is the basic form of the verb: *to run, to write, to become.* Splitting the infinitive means putting any words between the *to* and the verb: *to swiftly run, to carefully write, to quickly become.* Splitting the infinitive sounds natural to most people, and it should. The notion that infinitives should never be split comes from the influence of Latin grammar (in Latin, the infinitive is one word and can't be split), but no contemporary English-language authority endorses the total ban. In fact, not splitting the infinitive and preserving the intended meaning is sometimes impossible. *She asked me to kindly stop splitting my infinitives.* Putting *kindly* anywhere else in the sentence either changes the meaning or makes it ambiguous. Splitting the infinitive with too many words is awkward and should be avoided: *We wanted to quickly, forcefully, and with good arguments ban smoking in the workplace.*

2. You must never begin a sentence with *and, but,* or *because.* I suspect that this mythical rule comes from elementary school teachers who are concerned with style. A child might tend to begin every sentence with *and* or *but.* Beginning sentences with *because* might result in incomplete sentences. But you can begin sentences with *and, but,* or *because.* Because beginning sentences with these words is not an error, don't worry about it. Don't, however, overdo it.

3. You must never end a sentence with a preposition. This superstition also comes from Latin grammar and often does violence to normal English word order.

Consider these examples:

a. What did you wrap the presents in?
b. This is what I wanted to talk to you about.
c. Is that where you got it from?

Here are stuffy-sounding revisions without prepositions at the end:

a. In what did you wrap the presents?

b. This is the topic about which I wanted to talk to you.
c. Is that the place from which you got it?

Prefer a sentence with a preposition at the end to an awkward alternative. Ending too many sentences with prepositions makes for bad writing, but remember Winston Churchill's famous reaction to the rule: *"This is the sort of English up with which I cannot put."*

Note: ending sentences with *at* as in *Where is she at?* is a grammatical error. The *at* has nowhere else to go. *She is at where?*

Grammar Debates

Grammar and usage aren't always cut and dried. Here are some disputed points:

Taller than I/me

Most grammar books consider the following sentence an error:

Mort is taller than me.

The error here is the object pronoun "me." It should be the subject pronoun "I"—*Mort is taller than I*—because what the sentence really says is "Mort is taller than I am." But not all grammarians agree. Some argue that in this sentence, "than" is a preposition and requires the object pronoun "me." The object pronoun sounds more natural to most people, and there is no confusion about the meaning. Alas, the meaning is not always so unambiguous.

Look at the following sentence:

Jadwiga likes the snake more than me.

Does this sentence mean that Jadwiga likes the snake more than she likes me, or does it mean that she likes the snake more than I do? In this case to avoid the ambiguity, we have to fill the sentence out.

Over/More than

Some purists insist that "over" can't be used to mean "more than" as in the following sentence:

Over a thousand fans greeted the rock star at the airport.

Ignore them. This usage is well established and perfectly acceptable.

It is to be hoped/Hopefully

Many traditionalists object to the adverb "hopefully" as used in the following sentence:

Hopefully, Colbart will repay the money he borrowed from his blind date.

The objection rests on the notion that "hopefully" can describe either the speaker's state of mind or the manner in which Colbart will repay the money. But increasingly this objection is rejected. "Hopefully" here functions as a sentence adverb and clearly expresses the hope that Colbart will indeed repay the money.

Loan/Lend

Some, mostly British, grammarians insist that "loan" is misused as a verb in the following sentence:

Abigail loaned Mort the money to pay off his gambling debt.

The use of "loan" as a verb is not considered an error in North American English. But "loan" can be used in place of "lend" only to describe physical transactions. In a metaphorical sense, use "lend":

The painting lends the room a melancholy air.

Between/Among

English teachers and the like will sometimes insist that "between" is used for two and "among" for more than two. In fact, competent writers have violated this rule for centuries.

Here is a comment from the usage note on "between" in the *American Heritage Dictionary of the English Language*:

"*Between* is used when the entities are considered as distinct individuals; *among,* when they are considered as a mass or collectivity. Thus in the sentence *The bomb landed between the houses,* the houses are seen as points that define the boundaries of the area of impact (so that we presume that none of the individual houses was hit). In *The bomb landed among the houses,* the area of impact is considered to be the general location of the houses, taken together (in which case it is left open whether any houses were hit)."

Recognizing Clauses

Learning grammar is like learning refrigeration repair. At some point you have to learn the names of the parts. One essential piece of grammatical terminology is the clause. A clause has to have at least one subject and one verb.

Here's an example of a clause:

Ron sleeps.

Ron is the subject, and *sleeps* is the verb. I can throw in lots of other words and still have just one clause:

Ron sleeps at his desk during lectures on grammar.

Ron is still the subject, and *sleeps* is still the verb. The groups of words "at his desk," "during lectures," and "on grammar" are phrases. A clause can have more than one subject and more than one verb:

Ron and Pam sleep and snore at their desks during lectures on grammar.

Ron and *Pam* are the subjects, and *sleep* and *snore* are the verbs. It's still just one clause.

A clause that can stand on its own is called an independent clause. An independent clause by itself is a sentence. "Ron sleeps" is a sentence. So is "Ron and Pam sleep and snore." One independent clause is a simple sentence. Two independent clauses can be joined to make a compound sentence.

Rule One: Two independent clauses can be joined by a coordinating conjunction—*for, and, nor, but, or, yet, so*. (A handy acronym for coordinating conjunctions is *FANBOYS.)* When a coordinating conjunction joins two independent clauses, it has to be preceded by a comma:

Ron sleeps at his desk, and Pam listens to the lecture.

Rule Two: Two independent clauses can also be joined by a semicolon (;).

Ron sleeps at his desk; Pam listens to the lecture.

Rule Three: Two independent clauses cannot be joined by just a comma. This is a sentence fault called a comma splice. Two independent clauses with no punctuation between them is a run-on, another sentence fault.

Here is an example of comma splice:

Ron sleeps at his desk, Pam listens to the lecture.

Here is an example of run-on:

Ron sleeps at his desk Pam listens to the lecture.

Two very short independent clauses (fewer than four words) can be joined by a comma:

Man plans, God laughs.

Armed with this terminology and the three rules, insert commas or semicolons where appropriate in the following sentences. You have to decide whether each sentence is simple (one clause) or compound (two clauses).

1. Our dog Theo loves to go on walks and spray all the trees.

2. Reuben's dog Cleo loves to go on walks but she always gets in fights with other dogs.

3. Our friend Ursula walks Theo every day and feeds our cat.

4. Theo likes to drink water from toilets Cleo prefers to drink water from bowls.

5. Cleo and Theo sometimes go on walks together but don't pay much attention to each other.

6. Ursula slipped on the ice and hurt her leg so she hasn't walked Theo this week.

7. Ursula has cabin fever and is going crazy Theo is very restless and is growing impatient.

8. Theo sheds a lot so I have to brush him every day.

9. Our cat Izzy also sheds a lot nobody has ever tried to brush her.

10. We just bought new furniture and no longer let Izzy and Theo come into the living room.

Answers: 1. No comma or semicolon (simple) **2.** A comma after *walks* (compound) **3.** No comma or semicolon (simple) **4.** A semicolon after *toilets* (compound) **5.** No comma or semicolon (simple) **6.** A comma after *leg* (compound) **7.** A semicolon after *crazy* (compound) **8.** A comma after *lot* (compound) **9.** A semicolon after *lot* (compound) **10.** No comma or semicolon (simple)

PARTS OF SPEECH

Eight Parts of Speech

It's probably not true that we can't think about things we don't have words for. *Schadenfreude* is a German word that has come into English and means "pleasure derived from the misfortunes of others." As cognitive scientist Steven Pinker has pointed out, when people first learn this word, they don't suddenly acquire the concept of taking pleasure in others' misfortunes. They say, "Oh, you mean there's a word for it?"

Nonetheless, having words for things makes it easier to analyze them. Imagine trying to learn refrigerator repair without knowing the names for the parts of the refrigerator. "That thingamajig attaches to this thingy here and controls the gadget that regulates the temperature."

Traditional grammar classifies words into eight categories called the parts of speech. The eight parts of speech are an important tool for analyzing the grammatical structure of sentences. Here they are:

Noun – names a person, place, thing, idea, living creature, quality, or action. Examples: *thought, Hell, bazooka, dog, Leprechaun,* *stupidity, smoking, fork, licorice, wine, periscope, language, cat.*

Verb – describes an action or a state of being. Examples: *drink, fail, imagine, smoke, become, be.*

Adjective – describes a noun. Examples: *fat, thin, stupid, orange, hirsute,* (the articles *a, an, the* are also adjectives).

Adverb – describes a verb, adjective or other adverb. Examples: *stupidly, very, quickly, well, yesterday.*

Pronoun – takes the place of a noun. Examples: *he, she, it, we, they, someone.*

Conjunction – joins two words, phrases or sentences. Examples: *but, so, and, because, or.*

Preposition – joins a noun, pronoun, or noun phrase to some other part of the sentence. Examples: *on, in, by, with, under, through, over.*

Interjection – expresses emotion or surprise. Examples: *Oy! Wow! Damn!* (and many four-letter words I could never get past the editor).

Note that a word can be more than one part of speech depending on how it functions in a sentence. The word *smoking,* for example can be a noun (Smoking is dangerous), a verb (Ralph is smoking a pipe), or an adjective (Murray wore a lavender smoking jacket.) A good dictionary will indicate the parts of speech a word can function as and give examples.

Try identifying the parts of speech of the words in bold in the following sentences:

1. The singer sang, "I would **rather** be the Devil **than** be that woman's **man.**"

2. The **motel** didn't allow dogs, **so** we hid Bruno **in** the luggage.

3. Molly blew her **front** tire when she **hit** the **enormous** pothole.

4. I am **happy** to announce that the city will cover **all** damages caused by **potholes.**

5. **Maud** put her hand on her **heart** and **swore** that she hadn't touched the whiskey.

6. **Somebody stole** all the **zucchini** from the garden.

7. Victoria **has too many** flowers.

8. **Moderate drinking** helps prevent **heart** disease.

9. Because she **had** an **in** with the police, **Charlotte** didn't get fined.

10. The **President** should be **fluent** in at least **one** language.

Answers: 1. adv., conj., n. **2.** n., conj., prep. **3.** adj., vb., adj. **4.** adj., adj., n. **5.** n., n., vb. **6.** pro., vb., n. **7.** vb., adv., adj. **8.** adj., n., adj. **9.** vb., prep., n. **10.** n., adj., adj.

Adjectives and Adverbs

Adjectives are words that modify or describe nouns. Nouns are persons, places or things. The adjectives in the following examples are in bold type: *an **old** man, a **big** deal, **beautiful** Canada.* Sometimes two words are used together to form a single compound adjective. Some compound adjectives such as *part-time* and *old-fashioned* are permanently hyphenated and appear that way in the dictionary. Other compound adjectives are hyphenated—must be hyphenated—only when they appear before the noun, but are not hyphenated when they follow the noun: *a fur-lined coat* but *The coat was fur lined. A four-year-old child* but *The child is four years old.* Never hyphenated are adverbs ending in *–ly, –freshly brewed coffee,* and comparatives (–er) or superlatives (–est)—*a higher paid job, oldest surviving relative.*

One can make up a compound adjective, and when such an adjective comes before the noun it describes, it must be hyphenated: *He had a never-say-die attitude.* If you want to know whether a compound adjective is permanently hyphenated, that is, both before and after a noun, you have to check the dictionary. The adjective *time-honoured* will be there; *fur-lined* won't be.

Choose the correct word:

1. John was (wiser/more wiser) than his brother.

2. Of the two sisters, Jezebel is the (smarter/smartest).

3. Colbart's use of language is (most unique/unique).

4. The grammar column has (less/fewer) readers than the sports column.

5. A little (further/farther) up the street is a good vegetarian restaurant.

6. Discussing this matter any (farther/further) is a waste of time.

7. Whyte Avenue is (more quiet/quieter) now than it was during the playoffs.

8. John made the (most sincere/sincerest) confession I have ever heard.

9. Tofu is good, but steak is (more tasty/tastier).

10. The professor gave the (boringest/most boring) lecture I have ever heard.

Answers: 1. wiser **2.** smarter **3.** unique **4.** fewer **5.** farther **6.** further **7.** quieter **8.** sincerest **9.** tastier **10.** most boring

Adjectives have absolute, comparative and superlative degrees: *smart, smarter, smartest.* Most single-syllable adjectives form the comparative and superlative in *–er and –est: calm, calmer, calmest; tall, taller, tallest.* Adjectives with three or more syllables form the comparative and superlative with *more* and *most:*

1. *intelligent, more intelligent, most intelligent.* The two forms can't be mixed. One can be *wiser*, but never *more wiser.*

2. The comparative, *smarter,* is used when two persons or things are being compared, and the superlative, *smartest,* is used when more than two persons or things are being compared. If Jezebel had two sisters and was smarter than either of them, she would be the *smartest* of the three.

3. Some adjectives—*pregnant, perfect, unique, round, dead,* etc.—logically have only the absolute degree. No one can be more pregnant or more unique than anyone else.

4. The adjective *less* is used with non-countable nouns: *less sugar, less milk, less time.* When we're dealing with persons or things that can be counted, we have to use *fewer: fewer readers, fewer cows, fewer cups of sugar, fewer glasses of milk.*

5. & **6.** *Farther* refers to physical distance, and *further* means "additionally." Not all writers observe this distinction.

7. & **8.** Most two-syllable adjectives form the comparative and superlative in *–er* and *–est.*

9. Two-syllable adjectives that end in *y* change the *y* to *i* and add *–er, –est* to form the comparative and superlative.

10. Two-syllable adjectives that end in *–ful, –less, –ing, –ed, –ous* always form their comparatives and superlatives with *more* and *most.*

Note: In the case of two-syllable adjectives, it's a good idea to check the dictionary for the preferred form. For some, both *–er/–est* and *more/most* are possible.

Using adjectives sparingly

Mark Twain once wrote, "If you catch an adjective, kill it." It's good stylistic advice, although Twain was exaggerating, of course. We couldn't very well kill off all adjectives.

"What colour was the dog that bit you?"
"What?"
"The colour of the dog?"
"Uh..."

But using too many adjectives (and adverbs) is a common mistake of inexperienced writers. The problem with adjectives and adverbs is that they are often tacked on to a weak noun or verb when a single strong noun or verb without the adjective or adverb would produce a greater effect.

Here are a couple of examples:

Interest in the election **has increased dramatically.** – Weak verb modified by an adverb.

Better: Interest in the election **has surged.** – Strong verb.

Samantha adores **very tall buildings.** – Weak noun modified by an adjective, which is further modified by an adverb (very).

Better: Samantha adores **skyscrapers.** – Strong noun.

In the following sentences, replace adverb/verb combinations and adjective/noun combinations with strong verbs and strong nouns. Compare your revisions with mine:

1. Colbart lives in a **miserable little house.**
2. Colbart's ex-wife lives in a **large stately house.**
3. Abigail hadn't **realized beforehand** that such a **large number of people** would be at the theatre.
4. We **looked forward fearfully to** the beginning of the school year.
5. The drunk **walked unsteadily** toward his car.
6. Professor Snodgrass is an **extraordinarily significant person** in the field of kinetics.
7. The student **complained childishly** about his workload.
8. Bart's retirement party was a **great failure.**
9. The caravan drove into a **violent snowstorm.**
10. Jadwiga **looked steadily and intently** into Bart's eyes.
11. In time the country **will completely use up** its natural resources.
12. The election was a **spectacular success** for the governing party.
13. The magician **deeply impressed** the audience with his performance.
14. Bobby is a **highly skilled and knowledgeable** chess player.

Possible revisions:

1. Colbart lives in a **hovel.**
2. Colbart's ex-wife lives in a **mansion.**
3. Abigail hadn't **anticipated** such a **crowd** at the theatre.
4. We **dreaded** the beginning of the school year.
5. The drunk **staggered** toward his car.
6. Professor Snodgrass is a **giant** in the field of kinetics.
7. The student **whined** about his workload.
8. Bart's retirement party was a **disaster.**
9. The caravan drove into a **blizzard.**
10. Jadwiga **gazed** into Bart's eyes.
11. In time the country **will exhaust** its natural resources.
12. The election was a **triumph** for the governing party.

13. The magician **dazzled** the audience with his performance.
14. Bobby is an **expert** chess player. (Here a single adjective replaces an adverb and two adjectives.)

Several readers have urged me to explain the difference between adverbs and adjectives because they often hear them used wrong (or should that be wrongly?).

Adjectives are words that modify or describe nouns, which are words that name persons, places or things:

a **goofy** clown, **wonderful** Canada, a **vicious** cat.

Adverbs are words that modify verbs, which indicate actions or states of being:

The clown acted **goofily**. Canada did **wonderfully** in the World Cup. The cat scratched me **viciously**.

Adverbs also modify adjectives:

a **goofily dressed** clown, a **wonderfully diverse** Canada, a **viciously behaved** cat.

Adverbs also modify other adverbs:

a **really goofily** dressed clown, a **very wonderfully** diverse Canada, an **extraordinarily viciously** behaved cat.

Many adverbs are formed from adjectives by adding –ly, sometimes with slight changes in spelling:

goofy—goofily, wonderful—wonderfully, vicious—viciously.

Some adverbs are irregular:

good—well, and some have the same form as the adjective: **hard—hard, fast—fast, straight—straight, far—far, early—early.**

The negative adverbs *no, not, scarcely, hardly, barely* must not be used with a negative verb (didn't, don't, won't):

I didn't make no mistakes. Double negatives are a big no-no.

Remember that verbs such as *feel, look, seem, taste, smell* can be linking verbs that link nouns with adjectives, not adverbs:

She looks beautiful (not *beautifully).*

Most educated English speakers—especially human resource officers—consider using an adjective to modify a verb or an adverb a gross grammatical error. Imagine that the sentences in the exercise appear on your job application.

Choose the correct word:

1. I am not (real/really) sure why I was fired from my last job.
2. When my boss told me to take shorter coffee breaks, I didn't take it (personal/personally).
3. I don't always appear (calm/calmly) during an interview.
4. It is important to me to complete a job (satisfactory/satisfactorily).
5. When people correct my grammar, I try not to feel (angry/angrily).
6. It is not a good idea to play a radio (loud/loudly) at your desk.
7. You can (sure/surely) count on me to be on time.
8. Do you require employees to dress (neat/neatly)?
9. I (could/couldn't) hardly believe how hard I had to work.
10. Sometimes I answer (wrong/wrongly).

Answers: 1. really **2.** personally **3.** calm **4.** satisfactorily **5.** angry **6.** loudly **7.** surely **8.** neatly **9.** could **10. wrong or wrongly.***

***Wrong** is both an adjective and an adverb, and as an adverb it is mostly interchangeable with wrongly, but wrong as an adverb sounds, well, wrong to most speakers. In constructions such as *He was wrongly fired,* they are not interchangeable. As an adverb, wrong can't modify an adjective.

Conjunctions

Choose the correct sentence:

1. **a.** Martha was studying either philosophy or welding.
   b. Martha was either studying philosophy, or she was studying welding.
2. **a.** We have neither the money nor the desire to own a giraffe.
   b. We have neither the money, nor do we have the desire to own a giraffe.
3. **a.** Good grammar will both improve your job prospects and get you more dates.
   b. Good grammar will both improve your job prospects, and you will get more dates.
4. **a.** You must either read more or learn to make up facts.
   b. Either you must read more or learn to make up facts.
5. **a.** Good grammar improves not only your job prospects but also your digestion.
   b. Good grammar not only improves your job prospects, but it also improves your digestion.

Answers: 1. a 2. a 3. a 4. a 5. a

Nouns, phrases or clauses that are joined by correlative conjunctions—*both...and, not only...but (also), either...or, neither...nor*—must be parallel. That means that nouns must be paired only with nouns, phrases only with phrases, and clauses only with clauses. Of the above pairs, only the **a** sentences follow this rule.

1. In **a** the correlative conjunctions join two nouns—*philosophy* and *welding*. In **b** they join a phrase—*studying philosophy*—and a clause—*she was studying*. Also parallel would be "Either Martha was studying philosophy, or she was studying welding," joining two clauses. Remember that a clause has to have both a subject and a verb.

2. b is not parallel because the conjunctions join a noun—*the money*—and an entire clause—"do we have the desire..."

3. In **a** the conjunctions join two verb phrases—*improve your job prospects* and *get you more dates*; in **b** they join one verb phrase and an entire clause—*you will get more dates.*

4. In **b** the conjunctions join a clause—*you must read more*—and a verb phrase—*learn to make up facts.*

5. In **b** the conjunctions join a verb phrase—*improves your job prospects*—and a clause—*it improves your digestion.*

Prepositions

Choose the correct word:

1. Mr. Ringwallet divided the loot (between/among) all his friends.

2. After accidentally shooting his friend, Dick didn't feel (like/as if) he needed to tell anyone.

3. The vase fell (off of/off) the table and broke.

4. Has she been (into/in to) see you today?

5. The three stooges walked (into/in to) the broom closet.

Answers: 1. among **2.** as if **3.** off **4.** in to **5.** into

Errors in using prepositions are common. In the first sentence, if Ringwallet had just two friends, he would be dividing the loot *between* them. *Among* is usually used for three or more persons or things; *between* is used for two.

In the second sentence, the preposition *like* cannot introduce the clause *he needed to tell anyone.* The preposition *like* can introduce only a noun or a pronoun. *It looks like rain.* A clause—containing a subject and a verb—must be introduced by *as if* or *as though: It looks as if (not like) it's going to rain.*

In the third sentence, *of* is unnecessary. Similarly, *inside the house* (not *inside of the house*).

In the fourth sentence, the *to* goes with the verb *see. She wants to see you. She has been in to see you.*

In the fifth sentence the preposition *into* indicates movement to an interior location. The preposition *in* indicates a position or location. *They walked into the broom closet. They are now in the broom closet.*

Do you see anything wrong in the following sentences?

1. He strongly believed and was devoted to making money.
2. Inside of a dog, it's too dark to read.
3. Let's divide the oil between the three western regions.
4. She walked in the room and immediately walked out.
5. Stephen looks no better in a cowboy hat than a beret.

Each sentence has a preposition error:

1. The two verbs take different prepositions and both have to be included: *He strongly believed in and was devoted to making money.*

2. This is the second half of a quip by Groucho Marx: *"Outside of a dog, a book is a man's best friend..."* *Of* is often an unnecessary preposition. *The vase fell off* (not off of) *the table. All (*not all of) *the students passed.*

3. When more than two entities are the recipients of a division, the correct preposition is *among.*

4. She could walk around in the room, but if we mean *she entered the room* we have to use the preposition *into.*

5. Without repeating the preposition *in* before *beret,* we imply that Stephen looks no better in a cowboy hat than a beret does.

Pronoun Reference

Pronoun reference is an important grammatical concept. Pronouns always refer to nouns or to other pronouns. Without pronouns, we would have to monotonously repeat nouns all the time.

The pronouns in the following sentences are in bold type:

When **I** met Jan, **she** was walking **her** dog, **which she** had just bought.

Albert's cousin, **who** lives in Florida, loves to wrestle alligators.

That is not something **we** would ever think of doing.

The noun or pronoun that a pronoun refers to is called its **antecedent.**

Extremely Important Rule: Every pronoun must have one unmistakable antecedent.

An unclear antecedent is a mistake called **faulty pronoun reference.**

Here are some examples of faulty pronoun reference:

1. When Colbart hit his head with the bottle, he broke it.

What is the antecedent of the pronoun "it," the bottle or Colbart's head?

The sentence has to be rewritten, stating clearly what got broken:

Colbart's head: *Colbart broke his head when he hit it with the bottle.*
The bottle: *Colbart broke the bottle when he hit his head with it.*

2. Colbart and Jadwiga told Bert and Abigail that they couldn't come to the party.

What is the antecedent of the pronoun "they"?—Colbart and Jadwiga, or Bert and Abigail?

The sentence has to be revised to make the meaning clear:

Colbart and Jadwiga can't go to the party: *Colbart and Jadwiga said to Bert and Abigail, "We cannot come to the party."*

Bert and Abigail can't go to the party: *Although Bert and Abigail wanted to go to the party, Colbart and Jadwiga told them they couldn't.*

3. In the end Colbart and Jadwiga didn't go to the party, which was stupid.

Is the antecedent of the pronoun "which" the fact that Colbart and Jadwiga didn't go to the party (the entire clause) or the party itself?

The sentence has to be revised:

The party itself was stupid: *Colbart and Jadwiga didn't go to the stupid party.*

Not going to the party was stupid: *It was stupid of Colbart and Jadwiga not to go to the party.*

4. The cat's owners gave it away.

Although the pronoun "it" clearly refers to the cat, the noun "cat" doesn't appear in the sentence. A possessive noun (like "cat's") can't be the antecedent of a pronoun. This may seem like a very picky piece of grammar, but once you know it, you can feel smugly superior to those who don't.

The sentence has to be revised:

Don't use the pronoun: *The cat's owners gave the cat away.*

Name the owners: *Samantha and Bruno gave their cat away.*

Revise the following sentences to correct faulty pronoun references, and compare your revisions with mine. The pronouns are in bold type.

1. When Marg visited Georgia, **she** had a bad cold.
2. The contract's convoluted language will make **it** a hard sell.
3. Geraldine confessed to the crime and began to cry. **This** made Graham angry.
4. We banged on Bart's door, but **he** wouldn't open it.

5. Colbart and Murray use stupid pick-up lines that rarely work because women can't stand **them.**

Possible revisions:

1. Georgia had a bad cold when Marg visited her. Marg had a bad cold when she visited Georgia.

2. The contract will be a hard sell because of its convoluted language.

3. Geraldine confessed to the crime and began to cry. Her confession (or her crying) made Graham angry.

4. Even though we banged on his door, Bart wouldn't open it.

5. Colbart and Murray get few dates because women can't stand their stupid pick-up lines.

Spot the errors in the following sentences:

1. Every student should pick up their packets.

2. Somebody left his lights on in the parking lot.

3. Susan told Olivia that she was invited to the party.

4. They gave the manager a generous expense allowance.

5. I like that company because they have good labour practices.

The errors in these sentences are *pronoun reference errors.* Pronouns take the place of nouns, and they have to agree with the noun to which they refer (their antecedents) in number (singular or plural) and in gender (masculine or feminine). A pronoun must have one unmistakable antecedent.

1. The plural possessive pronoun *their* can't refer to *every student,* which is singular. The singular possessive pronouns are *his* and *her*, but neither by itself will do to refer to every student. One solution is *his or her own packet.* If using *his or her* seems too awkward, you can revise the sentence to read *All students should pick up their packets.*

2. Unless only men parked in the parking lot, *his* can't refer to *somebody*, so, again *his* or *her.*

3. Was Susan or Olivia invited to the party? We have no way of knowing because the pronoun *she* could refer to either Susan or Olivia. We have to repeat the name or make the statement a quotation. *Susan told Olivia that Olivia was invited to the party. Susan said, "Olivia, you are invited to the party."*

4. *They* is too vague. Who gave the manager the generous expense allowance? Similarly vague would be *They prohibit smoking in the office.* Probably the management or the boss prohibits smoking.

5. *Company* is singular, so the pronoun *they*, which is plural, can't refer to it. In fact, only the pronoun *it* can. *I like that company because it has good labour practices.*

Pronoun Case

The personal pronouns change their forms depending on how they function in sentences. When a personal pronoun functions as the *subject* of a verb (the doer of the action), it takes the form of the subjective case—*I, he, she, we, they*: ***I*** *know Mort.* ***He*** *knows Jadwiga.* ***She*** *knows Abigail.* ***We*** *know Abigail and Cecil.* ***They*** *know Cecil.*

When the personal pronoun is the *object* of a verb (the receiver of the action) or the object of a preposition (with, for, to, etc.), it takes the form of the objective case—*me, him, her, us, them: Mort knows* ***me****. I know* ***him****. Jadwiga knows* ***her****. Cecil and Abigail know* ***us****. Jadwiga and Abigail know* ***them****.* Note that *it* and *you* don't change their forms in the objective case. The objective case is also used after prepositions: *for me, with her, from them.*

Before an –ing form of the verb that is used as a noun (a gerund), use the possessive case *(my, your, his, her, its, our, their):* my smoking, your driving, our inviting, etc.

Errors often occur when pronouns are paired with nouns: *My brother and me went to the store.* To spot the error, drop "My brother and," leaving "I went to the store." The correct usage is *My brother and I went to the store.*

Whoever = he or she; whomever = him or her. You have to decide how whoever/whomever is functioning in its own clause:

1. Give the prize to whoever comes first. (*Whoever* is the subject of the verb "comes"—he or she comes first.)

2. Give the prize to whomever the judges select (*Whomever* is the object of the verb "select"—the judges select him or her.)

Choose the correct word:

1. Abigail assumed that her mother and (her/she) would be chosen Mother and Daughter of the Year.

2. Jadwiga and (I/me) love to read, but she likes mysteries better than (I/me).

3. (We/Us) grammar columnists live in mortal fear of being caught in an error.

4. If you notice any errors, alert the editor or (I/me/myself).

5. Everybody except (he/him) ordered chocolate covered bees for dessert.

6. Colbart's sister told Mort that she appreciated (him/his) telling Colbart to get lost.

7. Do you mind (me/my) smoking during the examination, Doctor?

8. The mugger passed up (whoever/whomever) was wearing scuffed shoes.

9. I will vote for (whoever/whomever) the party nominates.

10. Unlike (I/me/myself/), Samantha avoids reading the latest health studies.

Answers:

1. **she** – Drop "her mother and," and you have "she would be selected…"

2. **I, I** – The first "I" is the subject of the verb "love." The second "I" is the subject of the understood verb "like": …she likes mysteries better than [I like mysteries]. Unless she actually likes mysteries better than [she likes] me.

3. **We** – Drop "grammar columnists," and you have "We live in mortal fear…"

4. **me** – Drop "the editor or," and you have "alert me…"

5. **him** – "Except" is a preposition and requires the objective case.

6. his – It's not Mort she appreciated, but Mort's (his) telling Colbart to get lost.

7. my – It's the smoking that is in question. Whose smoking? My smoking.

8. whoever – The whole clause "whoever was wearing scuffed shoes" is the object of "passed up," and "whoever" is the subject of the clause.

9. whomever – The entire clause "whomever the party nominates" is the object of "support," and "whomever" is the object of "nominates."

10. me – The object of the preposition "unlike" is "me." The pronoun "myself" is reflexive and is used only to refer back to a subject: "I injured myself."

Choose the correct word:

1. The cat's howling is driving my wife and (I/me/myself) to distraction.

2. This problem needs to be resolved by the staff and (I/me/myself).

3. The organizing committee and (I/me/myself) would like to thank you all for attending.

4. Like (I/me/myself), you probably cringe when you hear pronouns being misused.

5. Three employees—Gladys, Hyacinth, and (I/me/myself)—were chosen to represent the department.

6. Only Hyacinth and (I/me/myself) actually attended the first meeting.

7. The big difference between my opponent and (I/me/myself) is that I tell the truth.

8. If you have any questions, please call Mr. Crabtree or (I/me/myself).

9. Either my brother or (I/me/myself) will be happy to help you with your garden.

10. The entire program was prepared by (I/me/myself).

Answers: **1.** me **2.** me **3.** I **4.** me **5.** I **6.** I **7.** me **8.** me **9.** I **10.** me

Britain has The Society for the Protection of the Apostrophe. I think we need to establish The Society for the Protection of the Pronoun Me. For some reason the object pronoun "me"—and to a lesser degree the subject pronoun *I*—is being replaced by the reflexive pronoun *myself.* I'm not sure why people are squeamish about using "me," but I've read some theories. One theory is that avoidance of the pronoun "me" is a result of hypercorrection. Children naturally use the pronoun "me" as the subject in sentences such as "Cecil and me caught a frog," which elicits the parental response, "Cecil and *I* caught a frog. Now, get rid of the frog." Formal English requires the subject pronoun after any form of the verb "to be," resulting in the stilted sounding "It is I." Perhaps some speakers can hear that inner parental voice condemning the use of "me," can't decide whether "I" fits, and end up settling on "myself" as a compromise. It's a bad compromise.

The reflexive pronouns—*myself, yourself, himself, herself, ourselves, themselves*—have limited uses, and it would be nice to preserve them. They are used when the subject and the object are the same: *I injured myself; You helped yourself; We served ourselves.* They can also be used to emphasize the subject: *I'll take the dog for a walk myself* (No one else will do it); *They took all the money themselves* (Nobody else took any).

People mistakenly use reflexive pronouns in combination with other pronouns or nouns: *Call my secretary or myself.* One way to hear the error and correct it is to drop the other noun or pronoun: *Call [my secretary or] me.* If "Call myself" sounds correct, it may be too late for The Society for the Protection of the Pronoun Me.

Choose the correct word:

1. The concoction was prepared by Dr. Jekyll and (me/I/myself).

2. Why anybody would want to be (he/him) is beyond me.

3. If you could be someone else, (who/whom) would you like to be?

4. The President's wife is more intelligent than (he/him), but who isn't?

5. Was it (we/us) they were talking about?

6. Let (I/me) go down to the station.
7. Everybody but Gerald and (he/him) laughed when I sang.
8. Tell us something about (you/yourself).
9. She readily gives advice to (whomever/whoever) asks for it.
10. (Who/Whom) did you say I have to call?

Answers: **1.** me **2.** he **3.** who **4.** me **5.** us/we **6.** me **7.** him **8.** yourself **9.** whoever **10.** Whom

1. No one would ever say, "The concoction was prepared by I." For some reason even some educated speakers often use the reflexive *myself* instead of *me* in such sentences. I wish they would stop. *Myself* is a reflexive pronoun and should be used only when it refers back to the subject or for emphasis: "I hurt myself." "I myself slew the dragon."

2. "Why anybody would want to be he is beyond me" rhymes and sounds funny, but it's correct. According to the rules of formal English, the object case of the pronoun (me, him, her, us, them, whom) cannot follow any form of the verb *to be.* Colloquial usage prefers *him.*

3. When deciding between *who* or *whom,* use *who* where you would use *he* or *she* and *whom* where you would use *him* or *her.* "Who would you like to be?" = "You would like to be who?"

4. The President's wife is more intelligent than he [is]... A minority of grammarians consider *than* a preposition (like *to, for, with,* etc.) and in such constructions treat *than him* as acceptable. You will raise fewer eyebrows among the rule-conscious if you stick to "...than he..." If the construction sounds too stilted, you can always throw in the extra verb: "...than he is."

5. In this case even traditionalists are in disagreement. The traditional rule requires *we* after "was it," but *us* as the object of the preposition *about.* It's probably best to recast the sentence: "Were they talking about us?"

6. All pronouns following the word "let" have to be in the object case.

7. In this sentence *but* is a preposition meaning "except" and requires the object case.

8. The reflexive pronoun *yourself* refers back to "you" as the understood subject of *tell.*

9. In clauses beginning with *whoever/whomever*, the correct form depends on how the *whoever/whomever* functions in the clause. Here *whoever* is the subject of the clause: *whoever asks for it.* In the sentence "She gives advice to whomever you select," *whomever* is the object of the verb *select.*

10. *Whom* = *him.* "You said I have to call him."

Choose the correct word:

1. Nobody hates winter more than (I/me).

2. She read twice as much as (he/him), and her lips didn't get sore.

3. I watch less TV than (she/her).

4. My wife likes the cat more than (I/me).

5. British Columbians wish they had as much oil as (we/us) Albertans.

Answers: **1.** I **2.** he **3.** she **4.** I **5.** we

The personal pronouns *I, he, she, we, they* have special object forms: *me, him, her, us, them. I love my dog* (I is the subject) *My dog loves me* (*me* is the object). In statements of comparison, object pronouns are often mistakenly used for subject pronouns because verbs for the second part of the comparison are implied but not stated. We can avoid the errors by mentally completing the comparison.

1. Nobody hates winter more than I (do).

2. She read twice as much as he (did).

3. I watch less TV than she (does). In spoken English the correct usage sounds stilted unless you include the implied verbs.

4. My wife likes the cat more than I (do). This sentence is ambiguous. Improbably, it might also mean *My wife likes the cat more (than she likes) me.*

5. British Columbians wish they had as much oil as we Albertans (have).

Choose the correct word:

1. They went (there/their) because (they're/their) boss told them to.
2. My recipe won first prize, but (her's/hers) tasted better.
3. (Its/It's) difficult to teach a cat to come when called.
4. My house is large, but (yours/your's) is larger.
5. (You're/Your) everything (your/you're) father hoped (youd/you'd) be.
6. (Ours/Our's) is the only house that was broken into.
7. This exercise (doesnt/doesn't) seem very difficult.
8. I (would've/would of) won the race if he (hadn't/hadnt) run so fast.
9. We bought a ('99/99) Honda Accord.
10. The cat knows (it's/its) master.

Answers: 1. there, their **2.** hers **3.** It's **4.** yours **5.** You're, your, you'd **6.** Ours **7.** doesn't **8.** would've, hadn't **9.** '99 **10.** its or it's (see below)

The words *there, their,* and *they're* are all pronounced alike and are sometimes confused. *There* is an adverb of place; *their* is a possessive adjective. *They're* is a contraction of *they are.* The apostrophe is used in contractions to take the place of the missing letters. *It's* is a contraction of *it is. Doesn't* is a contraction of *does not.* The words *not* and *have* can be contracted and joined to verbs. *Would've = would have.* Because of the pronunciation, the latter is sometimes mistakenly written as *would of.*

Confusion arises from the fact that the apostrophe is used in the possessive case of nouns—*the boy's bike*—but never in the possessive pronouns: *hers, ours, yours, theirs.* Apostrophes also take the place of missing numbers in dates: *A '99 Honda Accord.*

Sentence 10 is ambiguous. "The cat knows its master" means that the cat knows who its master is. "The cat knows it's master" means that the cat knows it is master. To avoid ambiguity, the second version should include the conjunction *that: The cat knows **that** it's master.* The conjunction *that* can be omitted following verbs such as *say, know, think: She says [that] she wants a raise.*

But omitting *that* can sometimes cause confusion. Contractions should be avoided altogether in very formal writing.

Choose the correct word:

1. Return the application to my secretary or (I/me/myself.)
2. Everybody but (we/us/ourselves) will be at the meeting.
3. Somebody like (I/me/myself) should be in charge of organization.
4. Joe and Anthony managed to get tickets for their wives and (theirselves/themselves.)
5. Our wives and (we/us/ourselves) will be going to the convention.
6. (We/Us) managers need time to think and relax.
7. We usually divide the free scotch among (us/ourselves.)
8. Either John or (I/me/myself) will give the keynote address.
9. Joan said that employees should address their complaints to Sam or (her/herself.)
10. If I talk too much, I usually say something that gets (me/myself) in trouble.

Answers: 1. me **2.** us **3.** me **4.** themselves **5.** we **6.** we **7.** ourselves **8.** I **9.** her **10.** me

The reflexive pronouns *myself, yourself, thyself, himself, herself, itself, oneself, ourselves, yourselves,* and *themselves* are used in two ways: 1) They refer back to the subject of a clause when the subject and object of the clause are the same: *I cut myself shaving. Gertrude taught herself Armenian.* 2) They emphasize the subject: *I myself made the cake. Olivia herself cleaned the cat's box.* Reflexive pronouns can't take the place of object pronouns: *She told me* (not *myself) to clean the cat's box next time.* Reflexive nouns can't function as subjects: *Myself made dinner.*

1. Drop *my secretary or,* and you have "Return the application to me." I suspect that some consider *myself* more formal in such constructions, but it's just wrong.

2. In this sentence the subject is *everybody,* and *but* is a preposition meaning "except," so the object pronoun *us* is required.

3. *Somebody* is the subject of the sentence. *Like* is a preposition that requires the object pronoun.

4. The reflexive pronoun *themselves* refers back to the subject *Joe* and *Anthony.*

5. The reflexive pronoun *ourselves* refers back to the subject *we.*

6. Who will be going to the convention? *Our wives* will be going, and *we* will be going.

7. The reflexive *ourselves* refers back to the subject *we.*

8. Drop *either John or,* and you have *I will give the keynote address.*

9. The subject of the clause is *employees,* so the reflexive *herself* is wrong here.

10. I don't get myself in trouble; what I say gets *me* in trouble.

Choose the correct word:

1. Ralph gave my wife and (I, me, myself) a rebate.

2. (Us/We) Albertans love to share our oil revenues.

3. Paul wants (us/we) Albertans to be fair.

4. Mary and (she/her) shared their rebates with John and (he/him.)

5. I suggested to him and (she/her) that they get their house insulated.

Answers: 1. me **2.** We **3.** us **4.** she, him **5.** her

Choose the correct word:

1. Nobody except (she/her) noticed that the furnace had failed.

2. Report any problems to the building manager or (I/me.)

3. My wife and (I/me) both like movies, but she likes comedies better than (I/me.)

4. (We/Us) homeowners have had a problem with ice dams this year.

5. Marion was surprised when her friend and (she/her) were chosen to lead the parade.

6. Teachers are always criticizing (we/us) students.

7. If you don't mind (me/my) asking, why did you wear your pyjamas to the concert?

8. The instructor called on (whoever/whomever) made eye contact with him.

9. They decided to support (whoever/whomever) the party nominated.

10. Much like (you/yourself), I find that red wine goes with everything.

Answers: **1.** her **2.** me **3.** I, I **4.** We **5.** she **6.** us **7.** my **8.** whoever **9.** Whomever **10.** you

Action and Linking Verbs

If asked to define a verb, most people would say it's an action word, which is true. *Jump, run, sleep, snore*—these verbs express actions. They're **action verbs.** But not all verbs are action verbs; some are **linking verbs.** You can probably get through life just fine without understanding the difference between action verbs and linking verbs, but understanding it will make you less likely to commit certain grammatical errors.

Linking verbs do not express action. What they do is connect the subject of the verb to additional information about the subject.

Look at these examples:

Aunt Edna is a kleptomaniac.
Aunt Edna seems crazy.
Aunt Edna feels great.

The verbs *is, seems,* and *feels* in these sentences do not stand for actions; they link the subject (Aunt Edna) to the noun *kleptomaniac* and the adjectives *crazy* and *great.* Linking verbs function a bit like an equal sign. A linking verb always links the subject to a noun or an adjective, not an adverb (most adverbs end in –ly.). No one would say, "Aunt Edna feels greatly."

Some verbs can be either action or linking verbs depending on the context. The verb *feel* is such a verb. Aunt Edna can *feel* (an action) the material in the sweater she's about to steal, or she can feel bad (she probably doesn't) about stealing it. If I said, "Aunt Edna feels badly," I would be treating *feels* as an action verb, and it would mean that Aunt Edna's sense of touch is bad.

Look at these examples:

A) *Uncle Sid grows corn.*
B) *Uncle Sid grows weary.*
A) *Uncle Sid smells the flowers.*
B) *Uncle Sid smells terrible.*

In **A**) *grows* and *smells* are action verbs; in **B**) they're linking verbs.

Decide whether the verbs in bold type are action verbs or linking verbs:

1. Edmonton **is growing** rapidly.
2. Samantha **grew** increasingly agitated.
3. Blindfolded, most people can't **taste** the difference between white and red wine.
4. Wine **tastes** better from a bottle with a French label.
5. After smoking a cigar, the child **turned** green.
6. Aunt Edna has decided to **turn** over a new leaf.
7. She **remained** at the party until midnight.
8. The mystery of the missing towels **remains** unsolved.
9. The situation in Karastan **looks** anything but hopeful.
10. We **looked** everywhere for the keys.

Answers: 1. action **2.** linking **3.** action **4.** linking **5.** linking **6.** action **7.** action **8.** linking **9.** linking **10.** action

Subject/Verb Agreement

Choose the correct word:

1. $25,000 (is/are) a bit more than I can afford to pay for a parrot.

2. Neither the students nor the teacher (was/were) sorry to hear the fire alarm.

3. Neither my wife nor I (am/is) planning to go to the party.

4. Neither of the clerks (is/are) able to remember the code number for fish lips.

5. The captain, along with all the team members, (was/were) caught placing bets on the other team.

6. Each and every dog and cat we saw at the animal shelter (was/were) grossly obese.

7. Each of five clowns (likes/like) to swim for relaxation.

8. The five clowns and their assistants each (hopes/hope) to get a raise.

9. Melinda is one of those women who (prefers/prefer) comfortable shoes.

10. Sam is the only one of those firemen who (doesn't/don't) lift weights.

Answers: 1. is 2. was 3. am 4. is 5. was 6. was 7. likes 8. hope 9. prefer 10. doesn't

Our ear is often a good guide to subject/verb agreement. Few speakers make the mistake of saying, "I does." A singular subject takes a singular verb, and plural subjects take plural verbs. Verbs that are used with *he* or *she* are singular; verbs that are used with *we* or *they* are plural: *The boy (he) walks. The boys (they) walk.* But sometimes choosing between a singular and plural verb can be tricky.

1. Sums of money are always singular.

2. When two subjects are joined by *neither…nor* or *either…or*, the subject closest to the verb determines whether it is singular or plural. Note that if we reverse the subjects, the verb is plural: *Neither the teacher nor the students were sorry to hear the fire alarm.*

3. Here the choice is not between singular and plural, but between two singular verbs. Because the pronoun *I* is closest to the verb, the verb must be "am." If the subjects are reversed, the verb becomes "is": *Neither I nor my wife is planning to go to the party.*

4. By itself *neither* is always singular and takes a singular verb. In this sentence *neither*, not *clerks*, is the subject.

5. *Captain* is the singular subject. Intervening words such as "along with" and "together with" aren't part of the subject. Two subjects joined by "and" require a plural verb: *The captain and all the team members were caught…*

6. *Each and every* is wordy expression, but it is singular and requires a singular verb.

7. In the construction "each of," *each* is the subject, and it is always singular despite the plural noun that follows: *Each of the five thousand refugees has* (not have) *received aid.*

8. When *each* follows a compound subject, a plural verb is required.

9. Here "who" refers to "women" and takes a plural verb. All the women prefer comfortable shoes, and Melinda is one of them.

10. Here "who" refers to Sam and requires a singular verb. All the other firemen lift weights; only Sam doesn't.

Choose the correct word:

1. Ralph is one of those politicians who (looks/look) good in a cowboy hat.

2. Stephen is the only one of the politicians who actually (wears, wear) a cowboy hat.

3. Paul, together with his advisers, (has/have) decided against a cowboy hat.

4. The number of politicians wearing cowboy hats (is/are) steadily declining.

5. A number of fashion decisions for the upcoming campaign (has/have) yet to be made.

Answers: 1. look **2.** wears **3.** has **4.** is **5.** have

Subjects and verbs have to agree in person and number (first, second, and third person singular—*I, you, he, (she, it);* plural—*we, you, they*).

Simple mistakes in subject/verb agreement are rare. Nobody says *I are, we am, I does,* or *he do.* You sometimes hear *he don't* for *he doesn't* in non-standard dialects.

Errors occur when the subject is difficult to determine. In a clause introduced by *who,* the verb agrees with the noun to which the *who* refers. In the first sentence, *who* refers to the politicians who all wear cowboy hats, and the verb is plural.

In the second sentence, Stephen is the only one who wears a cowboy hat, so the *who* refers to him, and the verb is singular.

In the third sentence, Paul is the subject. If the advisers were equals in making the decision, they would be joined to Paul by *and,* making two subjects. Two or more subjects require a plural verb. *Paul and his advisers have decided.* Words following phrases like *together with* don't become part of the subject. A wife, *together with (along with, as well as, in addition to, including)* her husband, **makes** the decisions. A wife *and* her husband **make** the decisions.

In sentences 4 and 5, the subject is *number. The number* + a singular verb; *a number of* + a plural verb.

Linking Verbs

Many readers have asked for further explanation of the error *I feel badly.* They have been taught that adverbs modify verbs and wonder why in this case *badly* shouldn't modify the verb *feel*? The reason is that the verb *feel* as it is used in this sentence is not an action verb, but a linking verb. Linking verbs are a special class of verbs that link the subject to additional information about the subject in the form of a noun or adjective complement. The noun or adjective *completes* the meaning.

Here is a partial list of linking verbs:

feel	become	the *be* verbs:
taste	grow	am, is, are

look	remain	was, were
smell	seem	will be
appear	sound	has been, have been
turn	stay	had been

Notice that many of these can also be action verbs. The verb *look,* for example, can be an action verb:

She looks carefully at the flowers.

Here the adverb *carefully* is modifying or describing the action of looking. But in the sentence *She looks beautiful, looks* is a linking verb that links the adjective *beautiful* to the subject *she.* The verb *feel* can also be an action verb. I can *feel* the texture of the wood. If I feel badly, it means that my sense of touch is weak. You can substitute a form of the verb *be* for a linking verb. *I feel bad* = *I am bad* (in a bad state). *She looks beautiful* = *She is beautiful.* This substitution doesn't work for an action verb. *I feel the texture of the wood. I am the texture of the wood??*

Try the following exercise. Choose the correct word and decide whether the word in bold type is an action verb or a linking verb:

1. Everybody **stayed** (calm/calmly) when the lights went out.
2. Bruno **waited** (calm/calmly) by the door.
3. The flowers **smell** (nice/nicely) this evening.
4. Her eyes **grew** (heavily/heavy) as she listened to the lecture on linking verbs.
5. Alonzo (careful/carefully) **tasted** the pyrogies.

Answers: 1. calm/linking verb **2.** calmly/action verb **3.** nice/linking verb **4.** heavy/linking verb **5.** carefully/action verb

Subjunctive

The subjunctive mood is used to express a command or wish or a condition that is doubtful or contrary to fact. The present subjunctive is used in requests, commands, and motions. The past subjunctive is used in *if* clauses that are contrary to fact and to express wishes, regret, or longing.

The subjunctive mood has almost entirely disappeared in English, but it survives in some constructions.

Here are the conjugations of the verb* to be *in present and past subjunctive:

Present

I *be*	we *be*
you *be*	you *be*
he, she, it *be*	he, she, it *be*

Past

I were	we were
you were	you were
he, she, it were	they were

Choose the correct word:

1. If I (was/were) you, I wouldn't bury that cat until it's dead.
2. I wish I (was/were) rich.
3. If she (was/were) in town, we didn't see her.

4. It is essential that she (is/be) on time.
5. I move that the project (is/be) terminated.

Answers: **1.** were **2.** were **3.** was **4.** be **5.** be

1. *If I were you* is clearly contrary to fact.

2. *I wish I were rich* (I'm not). The subjunctive is also used in such sentences as *If only she were here.*

3. *If she was in town, we didn't see her.* No subjunctive here because she might have been in town, so the statement is not necessarily contrary to fact.

4. This sentence would probably be better recast as *She must be on time.* But the phrases *it is essential, it is crucial,* etc. require the present subjunctive.

5. All verbs in clauses following motions are in the present subjunctive.

The present subjunctive also survives in certain set expressions such as *Long live the Queen!*

Gerunds and Participles

It is important to understand the difference between gerunds and participles. I can see readers' eyes glazing over, but let me try to explain.

A present participle is a verbal form (derived from a verb) that ends in –ing and functions as an adjective because it modifies or describes nouns and pronouns.

Look at these sentences:

Strangling an iguana, Susan smiled. *
The young woman strangling an iguana is Susan.
The gasping iguana was rushed to the veterinary clinic.

*No iguana was actually harmed in the explanation.

In the first sentence, the participle phrase *strangling an iguana* modifies or describes the noun Susan. In the second sentence, it modifies *young woman.* In the third sentence, the participle *gasping* modifies the noun *iguana.*

A gerund is a verbal form that ends in –ing and functions like a noun; that is, it takes the same positions in a sentences that a noun takes. Present participles and gerunds look exactly alike, but their function is different.

Look at these sentences:

Strangling an iguana is disgusting.
(Subject of the sentence)
I despise strangling iguanas.
(Object of the verb *despise)*
I object to Susan's strangling an iguana.
(Object of the preposition *to)*

Why is *Susan's* possessive? Because it's not Susan I object to, but her strangling the iguana.

A noun or pronoun modifying a gerund must be in the possessive.

We can replace the gerund phrase *strangling an iguana* with the noun *iguana* in these sentences and they will make sense:

Iguanas are disgusting.
I despise iguanas.
I object to Susan's attitude toward iguanas.

For practical purposes, knowing when to use a possessive noun or pronoun as modifier is the most important part of distinguishing gerunds and participles:

I see Joan smoking (participle); *I hate Joan's smoking* (gerund). It's the smoking, not Joan, that I hate.

Choose the correct word and decide whether the –ing word is a gerund or a participle.

1. We really appreciate (your/you) inviting us to dinner.
2. No one seemed to mind (me/my) leaving early.
3. The (employee's/employee) stealing paper clips was caught.
4. Perhaps (your/you) snoring at your desk was the reason you got fired.
5. (Anybody's/Anybody) sleeping on the job will be fired.
6. The (engine's/engine) overheating caused the car to stall.
7. The (man's/man) smoking in the third row is my brother.
8. We admired (Bob's/Bob) skilful skiing.
9. Bob saw (us/our) talking about him.
10. (Susan's/Susan) strangling the iguana got her arrested.

Answers: **1.** your, *gerund* **2.** my, *gerund* **3.** employee, *participle* **4.** your, *gerund* **5.** Anybody, *participle* **6.** engine's, *gerund* **7.** man, *participle* **8.** Bob's, *gerund* **9.** us, *participle* **10.** Susan's, *gerund*

NUMBERS

Only one of the following sentences is correct. Can you spot the errors in the others?

1. The printer accidentally printed 9 twenty-seven-page pamphlets.

2. Last month Colbart ate eleven pizzas.

3. 37 pairs of Colbart's socks turned up missing.

4. 450 demonstrators were arrested.

5. The gang has 22 members, of whom four are professional safecrackers, 16 are amateur thugs, and two are accountants.

6. Bernard was 36 when he was promoted to office manager.

7. Garth Szplstz, 46, was arrested trying to smuggle ferret tails across the border.

8. The meeting is planned for December 8th, 2049.

9. The last time the committee met was the 8 of December, 2007.

10. The knife was six and a half inches long.

Answers: Styles vary with regard to writing numbers, but the guidelines on the following page are widely accepted.

1. The printer accidentally printed **nine 27-page** pamphlets. When two numbers refer to the same noun, write the number in word form that can be expressed in the fewest words. If the numbers have an equal count, write the first one as a word: nine 9-page pamphlets.

2. Last month Colbart ate **11** pizzas. Numbers from one to ten are written as words, and numbers above ten are written as figures.

3. **Thirty-seven** pairs of Colbart's socks turned up missing. Avoid beginning a sentence with a number expressed as a figure. If the number can be expressed in one or two words, write it as a word.

4. **A total of 450** demonstrators were arrested. If a sentence begins with a number that cannot be expressed in one or two words, recast the sentence so that it does not begin with the number.

5. The gang has 22 members, of whom 4 are professional safecrackers, **16** are amateur thugs, and **2** are accountants. **Related numbers**—in this case, numbers referring to the gang members—follow the rule for the largest number.

6. Bernard was **thirty-six** when he was promoted to office manager. Ages that can be expressed in one or two words are written as words.

7. Correct. When the age appears immediately after a name, it is expressed as a figure.

8. The meeting is planned for December **8**, 2049. In dates, write numbers in cardinal figures (1, 2, 3, etc.) after the name of the month. The day is followed by a comma. An alternative is the military form without a comma: 8 December 2049.

9. The last time the committee met was on the **8th** of December, 2007. Write dates that appear before the name of the month after the article "the" in ordinal figures (1st, 2nd, 3rd, etc.).

10. The knife was **6 1/2** inches long. Mixed fractions are always expressed by figures.

STYLE

Clarity

Does grammar matter? Take a look at these two sentences from the **Plain English Campaign** website (www.plainenglish.co.uk). The first sentence is from an actual document on school children.

High-quality learning environments are a necessary precondition for facilitation and enhancement of the ongoing learning process.

Here's the plain English translation:

Children need good schools if they are to learn properly.

Which is the better sentence? For clarity, the second sentence is unquestionably better. Both are grammatically correct.

So, does grammar matter? If you never plan to write a term paper or have a job that requires you to write, probably not. You can make yourself understood without following the rules and conventions of formal English. If you make grammatical errors, a few snobs may think you're an ignoramus, but who cares?

If you are in school or have a job that involves writing anything that will reflect on your employer, you should care about grammar. But you can follow all the grammatical rules and still write gibberish.

Avoid the following like the avian flu:

Pompous, wordy alternatives to simple expressions

high-quality written communication = good writing

Silly, wordy euphemisms

We experienced a negative patient care outcome = Our patient died

Hackneyed phrases and empty "fluff" words

an ongoing process = a process (every process is ongoing)
an emergency situation = an emergency

Any phrase with more than one word that has a one-word equivalent

in spite of the fact that = although
owing (or *due) to the fact that* = because
at this point in time = now
gives positive encouragement to = encourages
is in direct contradiction with = contradicts
during the time that = when
in the eventuality that = if
did not succeed in achieving its objectives = failed

I know a very successful lawyer who says that he always tries to write briefs that his grandmother could understand.

Avoiding Clichés

I was on a bus recently and overheard a couple of teenagers having a conversation that sounded something like this:

"So, I'm like... and she's like...So, I go..."
"You didn't! So, she's like..... and you're like..."
"Yeah, no kidding!"
"Get out!"

No one could accuse these kids of being wordy. The staccato phrases were accompanied by facial expressions and hand gestures that doubtless conveyed more information than the words themselves. The ability to communicate this way is impressive, but it works only in a context of a shared and fairly limited experience.

Many adults do the opposite when they rely on clichés, euphemisms and jargon in writing and speaking. They use many words to convey almost no information. Take the ubiquitous expression *to have issues with* or *about something* or *someone.* I suspect the phrase comes from the counselling professions, where it may serve to soften a potential diagnosis. "You have anger issues about your mother" sounds better than "You hate your mother." The softening lies in the imprecision of the phrase. But precision is a virtue in communication.

Consider the following exchange:

"I'm going to order pizza. How about pepperoni?
"No, I have issues with pepperoni."

Unless pepperoni has an unspeakable effect on you, saying you have issues with it is silly. You might be allergic to it, or you don't eat it for religious reasons, or you're a vegetarian—whatever it is, it's better to just say it.

Good writers vary their vocabulary and use concrete terms that convey specific information. Clichés are words or phrases that have lost their freshness and meaning through overuse. Jargon is a specialized vocabulary that often includes unnecessary variants of simple words: *prioritize* for *rank.* Euphemisms can soften a harsh truth as a matter of taste, but some—*collateral damage*, to cite a famous example—are used to mask deadly truths.

Try revising the following jargon- and cliché-ridden sentences (You have to make up the missing information):

1. Costwise, the proposed restructuring is way off base.
2. The new secretary is a force to be reckoned with.
3. The bank executives have been getting a free lunch.
4. The dinner was awesome.
5. The lecture offered a meaningful learning experience.
6. At the end of the day, the university must become a centre of excellence.

Possible revisions:

1. The proposed restructuring is $5,000 over budget. 2. The new secretary is outspoken and extremely competent. 3. The bank executives have received billions in bonuses. 4. The dinner featured succulent curried lamb chops on a bed of quinces. 5. The lecture covered ten easy ways to save on groceries. 6. This sentence is meaningless.

Rules for Good Writing

George Orwell, the famous British author and journalist, formulated the following six rules of good writing:

1. *Never use a metaphor, simile, or other figure of speech which you are used to seeing in print.*
2. *Never use a long word where a short one will do.*
3. *If it is possible to cut a word out, always cut it out.*
4. *Never use the passive voice where you can use the active voice.*
5. *Never use a foreign phrase, a scientific word or a jargon word if you can think of an everyday English equivalent.*

6. *Break any of these rules sooner than say anything outright barbarous.*

Remember the difference between passive voice and active voice (rule 4). In active voice, the doer of the action is the subject: *John ate the pizza.* In the passive voice version of this sentence, the pizza becomes the subject, and John, if he's mentioned at all, ends up as the object of the preposition *by*: *The pizza was eaten by John.* Notice that we don't have to mention John: *The pizza was eaten.* Sometimes the doer of the action is known or unimportant, and it makes sense to use passive voice. *John Smith was elected President.* We all know who elected him. But usually, the active voice is better because it is less wordy and more direct.

Try applying some of Orwell's rules in the following exercise. Revise these wordy, convoluted sentences, and compare your revisions with mine:

1. A great enhancement of the learning potential of students can be realized by goal-oriented education professionals.
2. At the end of the day, production output will be maximized by a proactive managerial approach to effective interfacing with staff.
3. We need a staffing component that can think outside the box and cut to the chase in the face of deadline situations.
4. In the event that you have any questions, don't hesitate to bring them forward.
5. Adequate hydration is an important component of an exercise regimen.

My revisions:

1. Good teachers can improve students' learning. (Rules 2, 3, and 4)
2. Timely communication by managers will increase production. (Rules 1, 2, 3, 4, and 5)
3. We need staff who can think creatively and meet deadlines. (Rules 1 and 3)

4. If you have any questions, please ask. (Rule 3)

5. You should drink water when exercising. (Rules 2 and 3)

Each of the following sentences violates one or more of Orwell's rules. Try revising them, and compare your revisions with mine.

1. At the meeting, Harold raised a great number of important questions.

2. It is entirely possible that some of the calculations are in error.

3. A great many children exhibit a tendency to be hyperactive.

4. In an effort to be part of the solution rather than part of the problem, Jack has decided to tender his resignation.

5. We have considered all the available data on hedge funds.

6. Most of the demands made by the buyer have been met by the seller.

7. Reducing unnecessary wordiness, in my humble opinion, will greatly enhance readability of your essay.

8. The money we spent on upgrading the doghouse was nothing to sneeze at.

9. Miranda was happy as a lark when she heard that she had won.

10. The medical community indicates that downsizing average total daily intake is maximally efficacious in the field of proactive weight-reduction methodologies.

Possible revisions:

1. At the meeting, Harold raised many important questions. **2.** Some of the calculations might be wrong. **3.** Many children tend to be hyperactive. **4.** Jack has decided to help the operation by quitting. **5.** We have considered all the data on hedge funds. **6.** The seller has met most of the buyer's demands. **7.** Reducing wordiness might improve your essay's readability. **8.** We spent a lot on upgrading the doghouse. **9.** Miranda was ecstatic when she heard she had won. **10.** Doctors say that the best way to lose weight is to eat less.

(Sentence **10** and its revision are from the article "Logorrhea" in the online encyclopedia *Wikipedia*)

Parallelism

Parallelism is a very important concept in writing. In compound sentences and lists, each part of the sentence should be in equivalent or parallel form. Parallel sentence structures make the relationships between various ideas in the sentence clear. Sometimes your ear can be a guide because sentence structures that are not parallel sound a bit strange.

Here are some examples of faulty parallelism:

Not parallel
A president must be **articulate, resourceful, and always tell the truth.** (The phrase *always tell the truth* is not parallel with the two adjectives *articulate* and *resourceful.*)

Parallel
A president must be **articulate, resourceful, and truthful.**

Not parallel
He likes **biking in the mountains, exercising in the gym, and to work on his ranch.** (the phrase *to work on his ranch* is not parallel with the two gerunds *biking* and *exercising.*)

Parallel
He likes **biking in the mountains, exercising in the gym, and working on his ranch.**

Not parallel
The speech writer had to explain the policy **succinctly, accurately, and in detail.** (The phrase *in detail* is not parallel with the two adverbs *succinctly* and *accurately.*)

Parallel
The speech writer had to explain the policy **succinctly, accurately, and thoroughly.**

Revise the following sentences to correct faulty parallel construction:

1. To read a book about India is different from actually travelling to the country.

2. The new policy affected all managers, supervisors, and those involved in consulting.

3. Cat owners were angry and in a defiant mood when they heard about the new cat by-law.

4. To succeed in politics, you need not only to raise a lot of money but also you must spend many hours knocking on doors.

5. The warden said that Bert was a poor inmate because he complained about the food, completed his licence plates in a careless manner, and his motivation was low.

6. The principal is paid too little, obese, and a former prison warden.

7. Heavy smokers have a higher probability of coronary problems and of dying prematurely.

8. The restaurant was charming, the service great, and I've never tasted better food.

9. You are expected not only to organize the meeting, but you must also prepare the agenda.

10. Right now we should focus on researching the issue rather than on the recommendations.

Answers ***(Other revisions are possible):***

1. Reading a book about India is different from actually travelling to the country.

2. The new policy affected all managers, supervisors, and consultants.

3. Cat owners were angry and defiant when they heard about the new cat by-law.

4. To succeed in politics, you need not only to raise a lot of money but also to spend many hours knocking on doors.

5. The warden said that Bert was a poor inmate because he complained about the food, completed his licence plates in a careless manner, and lacked motivation.

6. The principal, a former prison warden, is underpaid and overweight.

7. Heavy smokers have a higher probability of coronary problems and premature death.

8. The restaurant was charming, the service great, and the food delicious.

9. You are expected not only to organize the meeting, but also to prepare the agenda.

10. Right now we should focus on researching the issue rather than on formulating the recommendations.

Active and Passive Voice

Anyone who has to do much writing needs to understand the difference between active and passive voice.

Look at the following sentences:

1. Gloria parked the car under the bridge.
2. The car was parked under the bridge by Gloria.
3. The car was parked under the bridge.

The first sentence is in the active voice; the second and third sentences are in the passive voice. What's the difference? In the active voice, the person doing the action (Gloria) is the subject of the sentence. In the passive voice, the object of the action (the car) is the subject of the sentence, and the doer of the action is mentioned in the "by..." phrase or left out altogether.

Passive voice always has a form of "to be" *(is, are, am, was, were, has been, have been, had been, will be, will have been, being)* followed by a past participle. The past participle of regular verbs end in "-ed." The past participles of irregular verbs are, well, irregular: swim—swum, eat—eaten, get—got (or gotten), and so forth.

A form of "to be" + past participle = passive voice

Why is it important to understand the difference between active and passive voice? It's important so you can avoid overusing the passive voice. The passive voice is not a grammatical error, but overusing it makes for bad style.

Look at the following examples:

Passive voice

In the book's first chapter the conflict between science and religion is discussed.

Active voice

The book's first chapter discusses the conflict between science and religion.

The active voice is generally clearer, more direct, and less cumbersome than the passive. Sometimes the passive voice is preferable.

Use the passive voice when the actor is:

1. Unknown: My car was stolen.
2. Obvious: Lincoln was elected president.
3. Unimportant: My car has been found.

But don't let the passive voice become your default voice.

Change the following sentences from passive to active voice:

1. It has been decided by City Council to have smoking in bars banned.
2. Mouse droppings in the cupboard were discovered by Gertrude, and Pandor was sent out to buy a mousetrap.
3. Many important issues are covered by the author.
4. Only one course of action is indicated by these results.
5. In the study a link between obesity and diabetes is established.

6. Many arguments in defence of smoking were made by the tobacco companies' representative.

7. A huge severance package has been given to the CEO by the corporation.

8. A balloon is inserted in the blocked artery and inflated. (To make this sentence active, you have to supply a subject. Who is doing the inserting and inflating?)

9. A rise in ozone levels has been experienced in major metropolitan areas of Canada.

10. The idea of putting a marinara sauce on pyrogies was conceived by Antonio Starchuk.

Answers:

1. City Council has decided to ban smoking in bars.

2. Gertrude discovered mouse droppings in the cupboard and sent Pandor out to buy a mousetrap.

3. The author covered many important issues.

4. These results indicate only one course of action.

5. The study establishes a link between obesity and diabetes.

6. The tobacco companies' representative made many arguments in defence of smoking.

7. The corporation has given the CEO a huge severance package.

8. The surgeon inserts a balloon in the blocked artery and inflates it.

9. Major metropolitan areas of Canada have experienced a rise in ozone levels.

10. Antonio Starchuk conceived the idea of putting a marinara sauce on pyrogies.

How to Write Obscurely

There are many reasons for writing obscurely. Perhaps you don't have much to say, but you don't want to be obvious about it. Maybe you have to defend an indefensible policy. You may hope that if somebody (say, your professor) can't figure out exactly what you mean, he or she will assume that you know what you're talking about.

Whatever your reasons for wanting to write vague, incomprehensible prose, here are seven strategies to help you achieve your goal.

1. Never use simple words: *I don't understand why cows chew their cud.*

Better: *My comprehension of the reasons for rumination on the part of domesticated bovines is of a negative nature.*

2. Always prefer passive voice to active voice: *I flunked the test.* (Active voice)

Better: *The test was flunked.* (Passive voice)

Even better: *The results achieved in the test were not acceptable on the basis of the standards that were applicable at the time it was taken.*

3. Always use nominalizations: Nominalization turns a verb into a noun that is then used with another verb to express the same idea. For example, "investigate the crime" becomes "make an investigation of the crime (better: the criminal act)."

4. Always keep the subject (doer of the action) as far away from the verb (the action) as possible: *We (subject) as far as possible under the circumstances prevailing at the point in time set down in the instructions provided to us by the committee will launch (verb) an investigation into the reasons for the failure.*

5. Always prefer two or more words to one: *Because I could not stop for Death/He kindly stopped for me.* (Emily Dickinson)

Better: *Due to the fact that I was not able to come to a full stop for death/He (Death) was kind enough to come to a full stop for me.* You can add the meaningless word "situation" to almost anything: *an emergency situation, a fatal accident situation, a celebration situation.*

6. Whenever possible use expletives: (No, not that kind of expletive! In linguistics an expletive is a word or phrase that has no meaning and fills only a syntactic function. *There were* and *it is* are expletive constructions. Sometimes expletives are useful, but sentences can usually do without them.) *Somebody ate twelve donuts.*

Better: *There were twelve donuts that were consumed by somebody. I need to go on a diet.*

Even better: *There is a need for me to reduce my intake of high-calorie sustenance.*

7. **Frequently use jargon that no one will understand.** If necessary, make it up. *Some scientific evidence suggests that taking saunas might be healthful.*

Better: *Taking saunas on a regular basis will promote the dehiscence of the chi by unblocking the positive field inhibitors that accrue in the subcutaneous areas of the soma.*

Try applying these seven strategies to the following simple sentences and compare your revisions with mine. Strive for maximum wordiness.

1. Good parenting can make kids more confident.
2. Regular meditation reduces stress.
3. Staff should feel free to bring their complaints to the meeting.
4. If you are not satisfied, please let us know.
5. We need to improve communication in our organization.

Possible revisions:

1. A great enhancement of the self-confidence exhibited by children can be achieved by effecting impactful improvements in the parenting skill level of the children's primary care givers.

2. The practice of meditation on a regular basis will reduce stress levels by negatively impacting stress-producing wave currents.

3. It is important that all currently employed associates who for whatever reason feel that they have negative feedback to share realize that the meeting situation will provide a non-threatening space in which their feelings can be shared.

4. In the event that you experience a negative satisfaction level, we would greatly appreciate your providing us with your feedback.

5. There is a need for us to bring about proactive improvements in the mode of communication utilized by all stakeholders within our organizational structure.

Wordiness

Wordiness is not really a grammatical issue, but it is an important stylistic issue. Many politicians, management consultants, and assorted bureaucrats indulge in wordiness intentionally. Short of setting legal limits on the number of words allowed per thought, we can't do much about intentional wordiness. But those of us who have no stake in obscurity can reduce wordiness in our writing by applying a few simple principles.

Take a look at the following sentence:

There were three grammarians who were strangled by a wordy bureaucrat last night.

The first thing to notice is the expletive. (e.g. *there are, there is, it is)*

Three grammarians were strangled by a wordy bureaucrat last night.

By getting rid of the expletive, we've reduced the sentence from thirteen words to ten. We can improve it even more by changing from the passive to the active voice. The difference between active and passive voice is easy to understand. In active voice, the doer of the action is the subject and comes first; in passive voice, the receiver of the action is the subject and comes first.

Active: I ate the whole pizza.

Passive: The whole pizza was eaten by me.

Let's change our sentence from passive to active voice.

A wordy bureaucrat strangled three grammarians last night.

We now have a sentence with just eight words instead of thirteen, and it's a much better sentence. Finally, we can eliminate the redundancy.

A bureaucrat strangled three grammarians last night.

Reduce wordiness in your writing by avoiding expletives and preferring the more direct active voice to the passive.

(I trust that the many politicians, management consultants and bureaucrats who write clearly and concisely are also good sports).

We can always improve our writing by reducing the number of words per thought. On previous page I have discussed strategies for reducing wordiness. The simplest strategy is to eliminate any word that adds no meaning. But conciseness isn't everything. Headline writers have to be concise, but they also have to choose their words carefully as this newspaper headline illustrates: **Iraqi head seeks arms.**

Revise the following sentences to eliminate redundancies and meaningless words:

1. We received an advance warning of the tornado that was coming.
2. One should in all circumstances be prepared for an emergency situation.
3. For all intents and purposes, we have completely finished the report.
4. Enron's total collapse was an unexpected surprise.
5. Virtually every separate case presented its own problems.
6. I have never had the actual experience of being surrounded on all sides by ravenous wolves.

7. Knowing the past history of the company, we can avoid repeating the same mistakes again.

8. Personally, I think we need an accountant who is honest.

9. In his brief summary of the report, he referred back to the basic essentials.

10. The philanthropist gave $30,000 of his own money to charity.

Possible revisions:

1. We were warned of the tornado. (All warnings are advance warnings.)

2. One should always be prepared for an emergency. (*Situation* is meaningless here.)

3. We have finished the report. (*For all intents and purposes* is meaningless; *completely* is redundant.)

4. Enron's collapse was a surprise. (Every collapse is total, and every surprise is unexpected.)

5. Every case presented its own problems. (*Separate* is unnecessary.)

6. I have never been surrounded by ravenous wolves. (You can't be surrounded on fewer than all sides.)

7. Knowing the history of the company, we can avoid repeating the same mistakes. (*past* and *again* are redundant.)

8. We need an honest accountant. (How can you think something impersonally? Would you say it if you didn't think it?)

9. In his summary, he referred to the essentials. (A summary is brief by definition, *back* is redundant, and all essentials are basic.)

10. The philanthropist gave $30,000 to charity. (Who else's money would the philanthropist give?)

Previously I discussed two strategies for reducing wordiness:

1. Avoiding expletive constructions such as *there is* and *there are.*

2. Preferring active to passive voice. *A wordy bureaucrat strangled three grammarians last night* is a better sentence than *There were three grammarians who were strangled by a wordy bureaucrat last night.*

3. Avoiding what is sometimes called nominalization. Has anybody ever suggested that your writing is wordy? Learning to avoid, or at least not overdo, certain grammatical structures will automatically make your writing more concise and easier to read. One such structure is nominalization. Nominalization turns a strong verb into a noun and uses the noun with a weak verb when the original verb itself is much better.

Take a look at this sentence:

The committee made an investigation of strangling techniques and came to a decision that bureaucrats should do exercises on their forearms.

The sentence contains three nominalizations:

1. *made an investigation = investigated*
2. *came to a decision = decided*
3. *do exercises on = exercise*

By getting rid of the nominalizations, we can reduce the sentence from 21 to 13 words:

The committee investigated *strangling techniques and* decided *that bureaucrats should* exercise *their forearms.*

Notice that expletives (there is, there are, there was, etc.) often involve nominalization and the passive voice:

There was great damage done to the American psyche by the attacks of 9/11.

The active voice without the expletive and nominalization produces a shorter, more direct sentence:

The attacks of 9/11 greatly damaged the American psyche.

Reduce wordiness in the following sentences by eliminating expletives, passive voice, and nominalizations:

1. It was decided by the committee that smoking should be banned.
2. All the cars were sold by the salesman who made the greatest effort.
3. We all have the ability to make improvements in our writing.
4. It is crucial that something be done about the use of too many words per thought.
5. There is a possibility that the woman who is giving the keynote speech will be late.

Possible revisions:

1. The committee decided to ban smoking.
2. The salesman who tried hardest sold all the cars.
3. We can all improve our writing.
4. We (or somebody) must do something about wordiness.
5. The keynote speaker may be late.

Using too many words per thought is actually a bigger problem than bad grammar in writing these days. In many cases, bad grammar—i.e., usage that violates the rules of standard English—doesn't affect meaning at all.

Look at these two sentences:

1. Jadwiga don't got no cigarettes.
2. Jadwiga doesn't have any cigarettes.

Both sentences are equally understandable. In this case, grammar is a sort of class marker. We assume that the author of the first sentence is uneducated. Now look at this utterance by former U.S. Republican nominee for Vice President Sarah Palin:

"My concern has been the atrocities there in Darfur and the relevance to me with that issue as we spoke about Africa and some of the countries there that were kind of the people succumbing to

the dictators and the corruption of some collapsed governments on the continent, the relevance was Alaska's investment in Darfur with some of our permanent fund dollars."

There are no gross violations of grammar in this sentence. Nonetheless, it is pretty much incomprehensible gobbledygook. It was of course spoken, not carefully written and edited. Let's try to come up with a sensible version.

Possible revision:

I have been concerned about atrocities in Darfur because Alaska has investments there.

Here is a brief review of strategies to ensure that your writing doesn't resemble Sarah Palin's speaking:

1. **Avoid expletive constructions** such as ***there is*** and ***there are:***

Expletive: There is a need for greater vigilance
Improved: We need to be more vigilant

2. **Prefer active to passive voice:**

Passive: A decision was made by the committee that a party be held to celebrate Colbart's promotion.
Active: The committee decided to hold a party to celebrate Colbart's promotion.

3. **Avoid nominalizations:**

Nominalization turns a verb into a noun and uses it with another verb when the original verb would do. For example, we can take the perfectly good verb "investigate" and turn it into the noun "investigation" and use the noun with the verb "make."

Nominalized: The police made an investigation of the crime.
Denominalized: The police investigated the crime.

Try applying these three strategies to the following sentences and compare your revisions with mine:

1. The layoffs caused a serious drop in the morale of the staff.
2. When there is too much haste, it leads to an increase of waste.
3. There are more than 20 students who made a contribution to the orphans' fund.
4. Mort gave a report on the problem but failed to come up with a solution to it.
5. It is unlikely that a dinner prepared by Ralph and his friends will be appreciated by the gourmet club.

Possible revisions:

1. Layoffs demoralized the staff.
2. Haste makes waste.
3. More than 20 students contributed to the orphans' fund.
4. Mort reported on the problem but failed to solve it.
5. The gourmet club will probably not appreciate a meal that Ralph and his friends prepare.

Conciseness in writing is a virtue. Previously I have discussed wordiness-reducing strategies such as preferring active voice and avoiding expletive constructions. An even simpler method is simply to cut out any unnecessary words. Trimming excess verbiage is an important part of the editing process. You have to be careful, of course, not to cut away so much that you lose meaning.

Years ago *Mad* magazine featured a cartoon in which the laconic American actor Gary Cooper was the UN interpreter for the Russian leader Nikita Khrushchev. Khrushchev went on at great length, and Gary Cooper translated: "Mr. Khrushchev says 'Yep.'" Given the Soviet tradition of speech making, perhaps no meaning was lost.

In the following sentences, try eliminating words that don't contribute anything to the meaning, and compare your revisions with mine. You may have to recast the sentences by substituting one word for two or three.

1. The family had a past history of alcoholism.

2. It is much easier to start over rather than try to revise the manual.

3. Chances are very good that students have probably not understood the assignment.

4. We have to give consideration to problems that may arise in the future.

5. The committee made a definite decision to hire a francophone.

6. We must decide whether or not to hold the convention in that city.

7. Abigail's behaviour is indicative of very low self-esteem.

8. Colbart had occasion to see three plays when he was in New York.

9. The prisoner was granted a temporary stay of execution.

10. No decision has been made concerning the matter of bonuses.

11. The candidate is pressing on despite the fact that the polls say she can't win.

12. Jadwiga carefully cut the pie up into six equal slices.

13. Ringwallet grew a moustache to hide a blemish that marred his appearance.

14. The philanthropist gave $100,000 dollars of his own money to the orphanage.

15. In the event that you can't attend the meeting, let me know.

Possible revisions:

1. The family had a history of alcoholism. (All history is past.)

2. It is much easier to start over than try to revise the manual. ("Rather" is unnecessary.)

3. Students have probably not understood the assignment.

4. We must consider future problems.

5. The committee decided to hire a francophone. (What would an indefinite decision be?)

6. We must decide whether to hold the convention in that city. (the "or not" in combination with "whether" is always unnecessary.)

7. Abigail's behaviour indicates very low self-esteem.

8. Colbart saw three plays when he was in New York.

9. The prisoner was granted a stay of execution. (All stays of execution are temporary.)

10. No decision has been made about bonuses.

11. The candidate is pressing on even though the polls say she can't win.

12. Jadwiga carefully cut the pie into six equal slices. ("Up" here is redundant.)

13. Ringwallet grew a moustache to hide a blemish. (A blemish mars one's appearance by definition.)

14. The philanthropist gave $100,000 to the orphanage. ("Dollars of his own money" is redundant. Who else's money would the philanthropist give?)

15. If you can't attend the meeting, tell me.

Here is another example of a highly nominalized sentence:

It is my intention to give a demonstration of how the avoidance of the nominalization of verbs can be achieved.

The following nominalizations occur in the sentence:

I intend becomes *it is my intention.*
To demonstrate becomes *to give a demonstration.*
How to avoid becomes *how avoidance can be achieved.*
Nominalize becomes *Nominalization.*

Here is a denominalized version of the same sentence:

I intend to demonstrate how to avoid nominalizing verbs.

The denominalized version of the sentence has 11 fewer words.

Here is an even more highly nominalized sentence:

In the absence of a demonstrated ability on the part of the borrower to make repayment, decisions in regard to the making of a loan will rest solely with the chief loan officer.

Here is a denominalized version:

Only the chief loan officer will decide whether to lend money to a borrower who cannot demonstrate that he or she can repay the loan.

Nominalizations are not always bad, but too much nominalization makes for plodding prose.

Denominalize the following sentences and compare your revisions with mine:

1. It is our expectation that staff will give management advance information about travel plans.
2. The committee reached a decision to give consideration to Bert's proposal that an extension of the search be made.
3. Colbart will make an effort to bring his coffee breaks to an end closer to fifteen minutes allotted for coffee breaks.
4. Regarding their party, Mort and Jadwiga have come to an agreement not to extend an invitation to Colbart.
5. The boys gave no explanation of how the breakage of the window had occurred.
6. It was essential that the young man arrive at an acceptance of his limitations if he was to have any hope of achieving survival in the real world.
7. There is a need for a re-evaluation of our office procedures.
8. He constructed a definition of the problem that was so broad that it robbed it of any meaning.
9. Failure on your part to follow the directions may result in the rejection of your application.

Possible revisions:

1. We expect staff to advise management of travel plans.

2. The committee decided to consider Bert's proposal to extend the search.

3. Colbart will try to keep his coffee breaks to fifteen minutes.

4. Mort and Jadwiga have agreed not to invite Colbart to their party.

5. The boys didn't explain how the window got broken.

6. The young man must accept his limitations if he hopes to survive in the real world.

7. We need to re-evaluate our office procedures.

8. He defined the problem so broadly that it was meaningless.

9. If you don't follow directions, your application may be rejected.

Gender-Neutral Language

Anyone who writes these days eventually confronts the issue of gender-neutral language. The trickiest aspect of using gender neutral language is pronoun/antecedent agreement. The *antecedent* is simply the word or words a pronoun refers to.

Take a look at these sentences:

John loves *his* dog. (The singular masculine pronoun *his* refers to its antecedent, the singular masculine noun *John.*)

Jane loves *her* cat. (The singular feminine pronoun *her* refers to its antecedent, the singular feminine noun *Jane.*)

Jane and *John* love *their* pets. (The plural genderless pronoun *their* refers to its plural antecedent, the two nouns *John* and *Jane.*)

Wal-Mart loves *its* employees. (The singular neuter pronoun *its* refers to its antecedent, the singular neuter noun *Wal-Mart.)*

These grammatically correct sentences follow the rule that pronouns must agree with their antecedents in number (singular or plural) and when possible, in gender (feminine, masculine, or neuter). Plural pronouns and the pronoun *you/your,* whether singular or plural, don't show gender.

Now take a look at these sentences:

A *doctor* has to care for *his* patients
A *student* should remember to do *his* homework.
Somebody left *his* car lights on.

In each sentence, the singular masculine pronoun *his* agrees in number with its singular antecedent, but what about gender?

All doctors, students and persons are not masculine.

This use of the masculine pronoun was long the accepted practice, but more enlightened attitudes toward women and concerns about gender equality have rendered the usage widely unacceptable. What to do?

You have five options:

1. You can follow the old practice and use the masculine pronoun. This option is fine if you write only in your diary.
2. You can use both pronouns: *A doctor must care for his or her patients.* Using both pronouns can get clumsy if you have to do it very often in a single document.
3. You can make the antecedent plural, eliminating the need for gender-specific pronouns: *Doctors must care for their patients.* This option doesn't work for the third sentence because the indefinite pronoun *somebody* can't be made plural.
4. You can omit the pronoun: *A doctor has to care for patients.* This option alters the original meaning slightly.
5. You can ignore agreement in number and use the plural pronoun *their. A doctor has to care for their patients.* This option is

common in spoken English, especially when a singular indefinite pronoun is the antecedent: *Somebody left their car lights on.* Although using *their* to refer to a single antecedent is still widely considered an error in formal English, it has its proponents. If you choose this option, many will assume you are making an unconscious error.

Word Choice

Choose the correct word:

1. These days many people have two or more (part-time/part time) jobs.

2. Jonathan worked only (part-time/part time) because he didn't need much money.

3. The Krugermar sofa was very (old-fashioned/old fashioned).

4. Jane bought a (fur-lined/fur lined) coat.

5. The coat Jane bought was (fur-lined/fur lined).

6. We thought he was a (six-year-old/six year old) child, but he was only (four-years-old/four years old).

7. The shop did an (out-of-warranty/out of warranty) repair.

8. We had to pay for the repair because it was (out-of-warranty/out of warranty).

9. The hostess served (freshly-brewed/freshly brewed) coffee.

10. You should look for a (higher-paid/higher paid) position.

Answers: 1. part-time **2.** part-time **3.** old-fashioned **4.** fur-lined **5.** fur lined **6.** six-year-old, four years old **7.** out-of-warranty **8.** out of warranty **9.** freshly brewed **10.** higher paid

Choose the correct word:

1. Sedgewick asked Wanda for a few hairs from her eyebrow as a (momento/memento) of their first and, as it turned out, last date.

2. George tried reading the history of Iraq but found the subject too (abstruse/obtuse).

3. Dick always (toes/tows) the party line.

4. Cecil's family traces its roots to (The Ukraine/Ukraine).

5. When it comes to ant colonies, Digby is (somewhat/something) of a pedant.

6. When Penelope (furrowed/furled) her brow, it indicated confusion, not deep thought.

7. Samantha soon became bored (of/with) meditation because her mind always went blank.

8. The Hebrew word *shalom* (denotes/connotes) "peace."

9. Ronald Ryan, convicted of the murder of George Hodson, was the last man (hanged/hung) in Australia.

10. Dorothea (lay/laid) her knapsack on a rock and (lay/laid) down to take a nap.

11. Farnworth was a (stanch/staunch) supporter of the husbands' rights movement.

12. After repeatedly winning chess games played with opponents recovering from surgery, Garth became too (complacent/complaisant) for tournament play.

13. Chris strove to make sure the distribution of Christmas gifts among his children was (equable/equitable).

14. The (lightening/lightning) caught them (unaware/unawares).

15. You can't go to bed (until/till) you finish the *How to Avoid Grammar Gaffes Once and for All* quiz.

Answers:

1. Memento – *Momento* is not in the dictionary.

2. Abstruse – A difficult subject is abstruse. One who finds even simple subjects difficult is obtuse.

3. Toes – The word implies keeping one's toes on a line.

4. Ukraine – Ukrainians prefer the name of the country in English without the article. *The Ukraine* sounds as if the country is a mere geographical region. *Ukraine* without the article is now standard in all major English-language publications.

5. Something – One can be somewhat pedantic, but the expression is always "something of a..."

6. Furrowed – One can furl or unfurl a flag, but not a brow.

7. Of – One is tired of something, but bored *with* it.

8. Denotes – To connote is to conjure up associations and images. *Shalom* may connote the Holy Land, but it denotes (means) "peace."

9. Hanged – Pictures are hung; people are hanged.

10. Laid, lay – Today I lay the knapsack down; yesterday I laid the knapsack down; Today I lie down for a nap; yesterday I lay down for a nap.

11. Staunch – Staunch means "firm or loyal." *Stanch* means "to stop the flow of something." *He applied a tourniquet to stanch the flow of blood.*

12. Complacent – *Complacent* means "overly contented or self-satisfied." *Complaisant* means "eager to please." Just to confuse matters, *complacent* can also mean "eager to please," but it usually isn't used that way.

13. Equitable – *Equable* means "unchanging"; *equitable* means "fair."

14. Lightning, unawares – *Lightening* is from the verb *to lighten*, which means "to make brighter" or "to make lighter in weight." Lightning is a noun referring to an electrical charge in the sky. It is also a verb: *It lightened several times last night. Unaware* is an adjective meaning "not aware": "He was unaware of the dog's presence." *Unawares* is an adverb meaning "by surprise" or "without warning".

15. Until or **till** – These words are interchangeable, although *until* is more common as the first word in a sentence. Contrary to popular belief, *till* is not a shortening of *until* and should not be written with an apostrophe ('till).

Choose the correct word:

1. Cecil's spiritual adviser urged Cecil to avoid the porn shop by taking an (alternative/alternate) route to work.
2. Colbart was not (adverse/averse) to cheating at solitaire.
3. Abigail was (loath/loathe) to try the fried grasshoppers Mort was raving about.
4. (Your/You're) more than welcome.

5. By the time Garth managed to raise his hand, Samantha had (all ready/already) answered the question.

6. Even the whiskey barbecue sauce didn't (titillate/titivate) her appetite.

7. Bert's uncle was an (eminent/imminent) authority on the sexual habits of water beetles.

8. Gloria's late husband thought that mixing pipe tobacco and gun powder for easy lighting was an (ingenious/ingenuous) idea.

9. Try not to (lose/loose) your temper when pedestrians push the walk button.

10. Ernie's excuses for never being on time were entirely (fictitious/fictional).

11. Jadwiga strongly identified with the (heroin/heroine) of the novel.

12. Dante describes the torments of the (damned/dammed) in great detail.

13. The prospect of ending up in Hell never (fazed/phased) Uncle Gurland.

14. Marion's aunt, a lifelong kleptomaniac, managed to (allude/elude) store detectives for forty years.

15. Bart suspected that the rags soaked in gasoline were (flammable/inflammable).

Answers:

1. **Alternative** – Actually, in North American usage, *alternate* and *alternative* are used synonymously as adjectives meaning "a substitute." In the UK *alternative* is preferred. In the sense of "every other" only *alternate* is acceptable: "The Grammar Gaffes newspaper column" appears on alternate Fridays.

2. **Averse** – To be averse to something is to have a strong aversion toward it. *Adverse* means "difficult" as in "adverse circumstances."

3. **Loath** – The adjective *loath* means "reluctant"; the verb *loathe* means to dislike intensely.

4. **You're** – You're = You are.

5. **Already** – The two-word *all ready* means "completely prepared."

6. **Titillate** – *Titillate* means "to stimulate"; *titivate* means "to decorate or spruce up" as in the dashboard of the car was titivated with red and yellow pinstripes."

7. **Eminent** – *Eminent* means "prominent or famous"; *imminent* means "threatening" as in "imminent death."

8. **Ingenious** – *Ingenuous* means "innocent or childlike."

9. **Lose** – The verb *to lose* has a *z* sound. The adjective loose has an *s* sound: The ferret runs loose.

10. **Fictitious** – *Fictitious* means false in the sense of dishonest. *Fictional* refers to fiction in the sense of creative writing.

11. **Heroine** – Heroin is the drug.

12. **Damned** – *Dammed* means "restrained by a dam, blocked."

13. **Faze** – If something fazes you, it bothers you. You can phase in better habits.

14. **Elude** – One eludes (avoids) danger (or the police); one alludes (refers indirectly) to something.

15. **Flammable or inflammable** – Oddly, these seeming opposites are synonymous and mean "capable of being easily ignited." Something that isn't capable of being easily ignited is nonflammable.

Choose the correct word:

1. How can we (affect/effect) changes in the cat's eating habits?

2. All that was left of the canary was one yellow feather (laying/lying) on the carpet.

3. Garth found it hard to (accept/except) responsibility for the cat's behaviour.

4. If the dog could talk, it would have (a lot/alot) of suggestions.

5. Before he got a cat, the old monk (led/lead) a life of quiet contemplation.

6. By the sixth sentence, the cat theme had (all ready/already) been exhausted.

7. Abigail hated to (loose/lose) at chess, so she loved playing chess with Colbart.

8. Colbart's (principle/principal) reason for playing chess was to see Abigail.

9. Abigail never felt the need to (pour/pore) over chess books before playing with Colbart.

10. Colbart's brain seemed to have a (porous/pourous) quality that Abigail valued.

Answers: 1. effect **2.** lying **3.** accept **4.** a lot **5.** led **6.** already **7.** lose **8.** principal **9.** pore **10.** porous

These are all frequently confused words:

1. *Affect* is a verb meaning "to have an effect on." There is also a rather obscure noun *affect* meaning "a feeling or emotion, especially as manifested by facial expression or body language." In addition to being a noun, *effect* is a verb meaning "to bring about," and that's how it's used here.

2. *Lay* and *lie* are so frequently confused that maintaining the distinction between them may be futile. *Lay* is transitive, i.e., it takes an object. You can lay the books on the table. I laid them there yesterday. *Lie* is intransitive, i.e., it doesn't take an object. The books lie on the table. I am going to lie down for a nap. One source of confusion is that the past tense of *lie* is *lay.* Interestingly, somebody who lies about is a layabout.

3. *Accept* is a verb that means "to receive willingly." *Except* is a preposition that means "with the exception of."

4. A lot of people believe "alot" is a legitimate word, but it's not.

5. The past tense of the verb "lead" is "led." Because the metal "lead" is pronounced like "led," some are misled into thinking that it's also the past tense of lead.

6. The two-word *all ready* means "completely prepared."

7. The verb *to lose* (rhymes with "shoes) means to "fail to win" or "to misplace." The adjective *loose* (rhymes with moose" means "not fastened tightly" or "not fitting tightly."

8. As an adjective, *principal* means "main"; as a noun it means "a person holding a high office" like the principal of a school.

9. You can pour yourself a cup of coffee as you pore over the morning newspaper.

10. The adjective *porous* is from the noun *pore*, "a minute opening in tissue." Abigail assumed that knowledge of chess might be seeping through the pores in Colbart's brain. "Pourous" is not found in any dictionary.

Choose the correct word:

1. We need an (extention/extension) cord if we're going to use the electric blanket in the backyard.

2. A majority of cat owners (was/were) opposed to the bylaw banning cats from public pools.

3. (May/Can) I borrow your gerbil cage?

4. While in Texas, we received (complimentary/complementary) tickets to an execution.

5. I have one (criterion/criteria) for owning a cat: it must be declawed.

6. Politicians rarely tell (barefaced/baldfaced) lies.

7. The constant need to (enact/exact) revenge for small slights is not a good quality in a clergyman.

8. If you (emulate/imitate) your friend's bad habits, you'll end up in jail.

9. When she cried, "What a stupid choice of colour!" she was (referring/alluding) to the choice of black wallpaper.

10. I always eat (less/fewer) cookies the day before the Weight Watchers meeting.

Answers: 1. extension **2.** were **3.** May or Can **4.** complimentary **5.** criterion **6.** barefaced **7.** exact **8.** imitate **9.** referring **10.** fewer

1. Many words end in the suffix *–tion,* but *extension* isn't one of them.

2. Fractions and proportions are singular or plural depending on the nouns to which they refer: *A majority of the panel opposes the proposal. A majority of panel members oppose the proposal.*

3. Traditionalists insist that *may* should be used to express permission and *can* to express the capacity to do something, but this distinction has little force in colloquial usage. Perhaps in very formal usage, the distinction should be maintained, but borrowing a gerbil cage does not merit a high level of formality.

4. Something given as a free bonus is complimentary; things that go well together are complementary.

5. Certain nouns of Greek or Latin origin have plurals in *a*: datum/data, medium/media. *Criterion* is one of them.

6. *Barefaced* is the only form that appears in most dictionaries.

7. As a verb, *exact* means "to demand and obtain by or as if by force or authority." One *enacts* a law or a part in a play.

8. To emulate is to strive to equal or excel positive accomplishments.

9. One alludes to something indirectly by suggestion. One refers to something directly and unambiguously.

10. Use *less* only with uncountable items—less sugar. Use *fewer* with things you can count—fewer cookies.

Choose the correct word:

1. Merry (Christmas/Xmas)!

2. (Seasons/Season's) Greetings!

3. What are you doing on (New Years/New Year's) Day?

4. What happens if the (elfs/elves) go on strike?

5. Didn't you give her the same present on (Mother's/Mothers') Day?

6. A box of beautiful (stationery/stationary) makes a nice gift.

7. This year I've decided to (forego/forgo) a third helping of Christmas pudding.

8. I (loath/loathe) singing chipmunks.

9. The smell of a roasting goose always (wets/whets) my appetite.

10. I thought it was my present. (Whose else/Whose else's) would it be?

11. (Thank-you/Thank you) for the beautiful poinsettia.

12. I (gifted my wife with/gave my wife) a dictionary for Christmas.

13. "How romantic," she said, with a (wry/rye) smile.

14. Our wonder at the stillness of the previous night was dispelled when the cat (drug/dragged) in a dead mouse.

15. Some Christmas shoppers need a taste (counsellor/councillor.)

Answers:

1. Either is correct. Many believe that the abbreviation *Xmas* is a secular denigration of Christmas, but it has been used in pious Christian writing for centuries. The *X* (pronounced as "H" in "he") represents the first letter of the Greek word for Messiah (pronounced Hreestos), which means Christ.

2. Season's Greetings (The apostrophe is necessary because it's a singular possessive— greeting of the season.)

3. New Year's Day = the (first) day of the new year.

4. elves (like the plural of *wife—wives*)

5. Mother's Day is a singular possessive, presumably because it's the day of each individual mother.

6. Stationery (*Stationary* is an adjective meaning "motionless.")

7. *Forgo* means "to do without." *Forego* means "to precede in time or place." The past participle is used in the phrase "a foregone conclusion." Hint: before ends in *e*; something that happens or is placed ahead of something else uses *fore*. There is a *foreword* at the beginning of this book.

8. *Loathe* is a verb meaning "to dislike something or someone intensely." The adjective *loath* (also spelled *loth*) means "reluctant."

9. whets = sharpens (A whetstone sharpens knives.)

10. Whose else (*Who else's* is also correct.)

11. Thank you (no hyphen in this phrase, which is short for "I thank you." *Thank-you* is a noun as in "I said my thank-you.")

12. Either is correct, although, as the *American Heritage Book of English Usage* points out: "Unfortunately, the use of *gift* as a verb in Modern English is tainted by its association with the language of advertising and publicity (as in *Gift her with this copper warming plate*)." *Gave* is probably the better choice.

13. *Wry* means "twisted or crooked." I like my *rye* straight.

14. dragged (*Drug* is a non-standard past tense of drag.)

15. *Counsellor* means "adviser." A councillor is a member of a council.

Choose the correct word:

1. The patient is feeling (all right/alright).
2. (Anyone/Any one) of those ties will go with the lavender suit.
3. The students were standing (all together/altogether) in a row.
4. The production of *Aida* was (all together/altogether) brilliant.
5. To succeed as an opera singer, you have to practice (everyday/every day).
6. The (principle/principal) ingredient in cotton candy is sugar.
7. The car was (stationary/stationery) when I hit it.
8. The orange curtains (compliment/complement) the lime-green sofa nicely.
9. Whoever decorated this room needs a taste (councillor/counsellor).
10. One should be (discreet/discrete) about personal information.

Answers: 1. all right **2.** Any one **3.** all together **4.** altogether **5.** every day **6.** principal **7.** stationary **8.** complement **9.** counsellor **10.** discreet

These are all frequently confused words, and computer spell checkers won't catch mistakes in using them.

1. *All right* is adjective meaning "in proper order" or an adverb meaning "in a satisfactory way." The one-word variant *alright* is not acceptable in formal English.

2. *Any one* means "whatever one (person or thing) of a group." *Anyone* is a pronoun that means "any person." *Anyone who writes need to study grammar.*

3. *All together* to indicates that the members of a group are acting collectively. *All* and *together* may be separated by other words: *All the students were standing together in a row.*

4. *Altogether* is an adverb meaning "entirely, completely, utterly."

5. *Every day* means "each day." *Everyday* is an adjective meaning "ordinary" or "casual." *She wore her everyday clothes.*

6. *Principal* as an adjective means "chief" or "main." As a noun, it means a person holding the highest rank, especially the head of an elementary school. In a loan, the principal is the larger part of the money, and the interest is the lesser (unless it's a credit card bill). *Principle* is only a noun meaning "a rule" or "a standard."

7. Something standing still is said to be *stationary. Stationery* is what people used to write letters on before email.

8. As a noun, *complement* means "something that completes or enhances" *The beautiful wooden chess set was a complement to the antique leather furniture;* used as a verb it means "to serve as a complement to." The noun *compliment* means "an expression of praise" *She paid me a compliment on my boots,* while the verb means "to pay a compliment to."

9. A *councillor* is a member of a council; a *counsellor* is one who gives counsel or advice.

10. *Discreet* means "prudent or circumspect." *Discrete* means "separate or distinct." *We divided into two discrete groups: bridge players and chess players.*

Choose the correct word:

1. The dog (lead/led) us to the scene of the accident.

2. The dog's behaviour (begs/raises) the question: are dogs smarter than cats?

3. When the dog was punished, the cat thought it got its just (deserts/desserts.)

4. The reason I like cats is (because/that) they're very affectionate.

5. I am (adverse/averse) to having a cat sleep in my bed.

Answers: **1.** led **2.** raises **3.** deserts **4.** that **5.** averse

1. The past tense of the verb *lead* is *led.* I am told that using *lead* as the past tense of *lead* is a very common error in university students' papers. The confusion probably arises from the past tense of *read,* which is *read* and rhymes with the metal *lead.*

2. *Begging the question* is a logical fallacy that assumes as true the point (question) being argued. Here's an example of begging the question: *Cats are stupid because they just aren't very bright.* No evidence is offered for the assertion that cats are stupid beyond restating the assertion in different words. Those who are unfamiliar with this special sense of *to beg the question* mistakenly assume that the phrase means "demands that the question be asked." It doesn't.

3. To get one's just deserts is to get what one justly deserves. A *desert* (accent on the first syllable) is an arid, barren expanse of land; the noun *dessert* (accent on the second syllable) is a sweet dish served at the end of a meal. A third noun *desert*—with the accent on the second syllable—refers to a deserved reward or punishment. So the dog got its *just deserts.*

4. Although *the reason is because* is very widely used, the use of *because* is considered redundant. It should be *the reason is that.* The sentence is probably better recast to eliminate *reason: I like cats because they're very affectionate.*

5. *Adverse* and *averse* are often confused. *Adverse* means "negative" or "bad," as in *adverse circumstances. Averse* means "opposed."

Choose the correct word:

1. How will the introduction of smaller paper clips (affect/effect/impact) your department?

2. The new CEO wants to (affect/effect/) major changes in the use of paper clips.

3. Aside from inconveniencing employees with large fingers, smaller paper clips will have no (affect/effect/impact) at all.

4. The new policy on paper clips was not very (affective/effective/impactful.)

5. To live dangerously, she (affects/effects) an American accent when travelling abroad.

Answers: 1. affect or impact 2. effect 3. effect or impact 4. effective 5. affects

The words *affect* and *effect* are often confused. Both are verbs. To *affect* something is to change or influence it. To *effect* something is to bring it about.

1. How will the policy *affect* the department? (How will it change or influence it?)

2. The new CEO wants to *effect* major changes. (He or she wants to bring about major changes.)

Affect can also mean "to put on a false show of," as in sentence five. *Effect* is also a noun. An *effect* is that which is brought about, a result.

3. The new policy will have no *effect.* (The policy will have no result.)

As a verb, *impact* means literally "to strike with a blow" or "to pack firmly together." As a noun, it means "collision." It is used as a synonym for both the verb *affect* (sentence 1) and the noun *effect* (sentence 3). Many object to the use of *impact* as a verb, but the *American Heritage Dictionary of the English Language* points out that *impact* has been used as a verb since 1601 and as a synonym of *affect* since 1935. The use of *impact* as a verb meaning "to affect" is very widespread in corporate culture, but it gives writing an unmistakable stamp of Management Speak. Unless you need to be fluent in Management Speak to climb the corporate ladder, prefer *affect.* Perhaps using *impact* as a noun to mean "effect" should be restricted to events that are more earthshaking than the result of a minor policy change.

The disappearance of a third of the Earth's population had a tremendous impact on the global economy.

Impactful meaning "effective" (sentence 4) is pure jargon, the invention of hard-core devotees of corporate gobbledygook.

Choose the correct word or phrase:

1. I feel (bad, badly) about gas prices.
2. Winston tastes good (like/as) a cigarette should.
3. Ten items or (less/fewer.)
4. (Hopefully/I hope) gas prices will go down.
5. I would (of/have) voted twice, but I was caught.

Answers: 1. bad **2.** as **3.** fewer **4.** I hope **5.** have

1. *Badly* is an adverb (most adverbs end in *–ly),* and adverbs describe verbs, adjectives or other adverbs. But here the verb *feel* isn't an action that *badly* can describe. If you feel badly, your sense of touch is weak. Here *feel* is a linking verb that links the adjective *bad* with the subject *I.*

2. Readers old enough to remember cigarette commercials will recognize the famously ungrammatical Winston cigarette slogan. *Like* can introduce a noun—*He talks like a politician*—but not an entire clause. A clause (with a subject and a verb) has to be introduced by *as, as if, or as though. It looks as if* (not *like) it might rain.*

3. We see the grammar error in No. 3 every day in the supermarket. *Less* is used only with non-count nouns: *less sugar, less coffee, less shopping. Fewer* is used with nouns that can be counted: fewer *cubes of sugar, fewer cups of coffee, fewer items.*

4. *Hopefully* is often used to mean *It is to be hoped* or *I hope,* but purists insist that it shouldn't be. Since *hopefully* means "full of hope," there is nothing for it to modify in sentence 4. The gas price won't be full of hope. Unless you want to drive purists crazy—and you might—avoid using *hopefully* this way.

5. Finally, in spoken English, the *have* in *would have* is sometimes pronounced like *of,* but we have to remember not to write it that way.

Choose the correct word:

1. When I heard about the accident, I tried to get (ahold/hold) of Jack and Jill.

2. Please keep me (appraised/apprised) of their condition.

3. The dog's constant shedding presented a great (dilemma/problem).

4. The lecture centered (around/on) how to get cat vomit stains out of leather furniture.

5. When it comes to obeying rules, cats are different (than/from) dogs.

6. The cat (dragged/drug) in a dead mouse and left it on the table.

7. Would you mind keeping my cat at your house for (awhile/a while)?

8. Around the cat, we try to be (discreet/discrete) on the subject of euthanasia.

9. As John was leaving for work, his wife said, "Don't forget to (bring/take) your briefcase.

10. Sara got her song (copywritten/copyrighted).

Answers: 1. hold **2.** apprised **3.** problem **4.** on **5.** from **6.** dragged **7.** a while **8.** discreet **9.** take **10.** copyrighted

1. In standard English, one gets hold, not ahold, of someone.

2. You can get your house appraised, but if you want to keep informed, you get apprised.

3. A *dilemma* isn't just any problem; it's a difficult choice: *Whether to keep the dog or give it away is a dilemma.* Technically, a dilemma is a choice between two equally unacceptable alternatives: Cedric had to take the poison or be shot.

4. A lecture can revolve around a particular topic, but it centers *on* one.

5. You can use *different than* only to introduce an entire clause: *She looked different than I thought she would.*

6. The standard past tense of *drag* is *dragged.*

7. *Awhile* is an adverb meaning for a time: *I lay down awhile before dinner.* After the preposition *for*, use two words: *For a while I couldn't understand what he was saying.*

8. *Discreet* means "circumspect"; *discrete* means "distinct": *I made two discrete lists of animals not to own: cats and dogs.*

9. Whether to use *take* or *bring* is a matter of perspective. From John's wife's perspective, he takes his briefcase to work and brings it home from work.

10. There is no such word as *copywrite.* To copyright something is to secure the rights to it.

Choose the correct word:

1. The cat has (laid/lain) on the pillow since early this morning.

2. Last night I (lay/laid) in bed for hours, but I couldn't fall asleep.

3. We like to (lay/lie) around on Sunday afternoon.

4. They are (laying, lying) in the sun.

5. She (lay/laid) down the law: no eating cookies while (laying/lying) on the sofa.

Answers: 1. lain **2.** lay **3.** lie **4.** lying **5.** laid, lying

The verbs *lie* and *lay* are often confused, and if you can learn to use them correctly once and for all, you'll be part of a small, elite minority. First, you need to learn a couple of grammatical terms. *Lie* is an **intransitive verb**, meaning it never takes an object. *Lay* is a **transitive verb**, meaning it always takes an object. *I lie down for a nap* (no object) *I lay the book down on the table* (***book*** is the object of lay). When you *lay*, you're inevitably laying something.

Here's a source of much of the confusion:

The past tense of *lie* is *lay*.

Yesterday I lay down for a nap.

Take a look at the following chart:

Present	Past
lie	lay
lay	laid
Present Participle	**Past Participle**
lying	lain
laying	laid

Sentences using *lie*:

1. *Every day I lie down for a nap.*
2. *Yesterday I lay down for a nap.*

3. *I have lain on the couch all morning.*
4. *I was lying on the beach.*

Note that these sentences have no objects.

Sentences using ***lay:***

1. *Every day I lay the newspaper on the table.*
2. *Yesterday I laid the newspaper on the table.*
3. *I have laid the newspaper on the table every day for a year.*
4. *Where have you been laying the newspaper?*

Note that in each of these sentences, the object is *newspaper.*

Choose the correct word or phrase:

1. Having won the election, he thought he had free (reign/rein) to (reek/wreak) havoc on the planet.

2. The invasion turned out to be a (hair-brained/hare-brained) idea.

3. Occasionally foregoing donuts, Colbart began to (hone in /home in) on a solution to his weight problem.

4. The idea of getting a job to solve his financial problems briefly (peaked/piqued) Cecil's interest.

5. Steve thought he could get ahead by (towing/toeing) management's line.

6. Isabella kept Carlos on (tenderhooks/tenterhooks) for months before finally marrying Fernando.

7. We nipped our dandelion problem in the (bud/butt) when we bought a goat.

8. Colbart was in the (throws/throes) of a panic attack when the pizza finally arrived.

9. Our hearts sank as we (pored/poured) over Uncle Emmet's will.

10. Leaving all his money to the SPCA didn't (jive/jibe) with his well-known aversion to cats.

11. For Colbart, eating donuts and gaining weight had become a vicious (circle/cycle.)

12. Al's brother was diagnosed with (sick-as-hell/sickle-cell) anemia.

13. Many people have a recurring dream in which they're (butt naked/buck naked) in a crowded room.

14. Marianna was (chomping/champing) at the bit to get started on her career as a horse trainer.

15. Lady Macbeth got her just (desserts/deserts.)

Answers: 1. rein, wreak **2.** hare-brained **3.** home in **4.** piqued **5.** toeing **6.** tenterhooks **7.** bud **8.** throes **9.** pored **10.** jibe **11.** circle **12.** sickle-cell (Give yourself creativity points for missing this one.) **13.** buck naked (There is the expression "butt ugly.") **14.** champing (Look it up.) **15.** deserts (Shakespeare didn't describe any desserts in his play but she was probably getting them too.)

All these errors are eggcorns, a term recently coined by a group of linguists. The term comes from the curious mistake of writing "egg corn" instead of "acorn." An eggcorn is not just any phonetic misspelling (say, its for it's), but a misspelling or substitution that makes some sense, at least to those who make it. An acorn, after all, has roughly the shape of an egg. There is something appealing about nipping some problems in the butt. As a child, I long thought God had created one person named Adamaneve. You can read more about eggcorns by searching for "the eggcorn database" with your favourite search engine.

Before Terry Nadasdi, a linguistics professor at the University of Alberta, emailed me, I had never heard the term "eggcorn." Professor Nadasdi has developed a free online grammar and spell checker, **SpellCheckPlus.com**, that can catch many basic grammar errors and, amazingly, several thousand commonly confused words and eggcorns. I urge readers to take a look at it. **SpellCheckPlus.com** is a work in progress, and Professor Nadasdi welcomes feedback.

Spell checkers are notoriously unreliable and no one should rely on them exclusively. An editor I know has suggested that spell checkers have actually contributed to the proliferation of spelling errors because people do rely on them. In fact, I think my spell checker has made me a marginally better speller, but I always have my wife proofread what I write anyway. Until the technology is perfected, poor spellers should try to marry good spellers.

Choose the correct word:

1. Marion was not (adverse/averse) to buying high-risk stocks.

2. She was (reticent/reluctant) to discuss her investments.

3. The poet made frequent (illusions/allusions) to his delusions.

4. The pickpocket (alluded/eluded) the police by disguising himself as a nun.

5. Day dreaming was Maxim's (principle/principal) occupation.

6. I have (got/gotten) used to (loosing/losing) at chess.

7. Would you like (desert/dessert) before or after the main course?

8. I don't want to hear the (grisly/grizzly) details.

9. Such a good lead should have (lead/led) us to the culprit.

10. Bad (costumer/customer) service is often the downside of a booming economy.

11. John is doing (all right/alright) in his new job.

12. The evidence had no (affect/effect) on Mr. MacSheney's views.

13. The general will (martial/marshal) her troops.

14. The Mafia boss tried to (defuse/diffuse) the angry confrontation by shooting one of bookmakers.

15. I frequently seek the mayor's (council/counsel) when my car is stuck.

Answers: 1. averse **2.** reluctant **3.** allusions **4.** eluded **5.** principal **6.** got or gotten, losing **7.** dessert **8.** grisly **9.** led **10.** customer **11.** all right **12.** effect **13.** marshal **14.** defuse **15.** counsel

These are all frequently confused words:

1. *Adverse* means "unfavourable" as in "adverse circumstances. *Averse* means "strongly disinclined."

2. *Reticent* and *reluctant* are close in meaning. A *reticent* man is inclined to be silent about his thoughts and feelings. He is reluctant to speak but *reticent* **about** speaking.

3. An *allusion* is an indirect reference to something; an *illusion* is an erroneous perception of reality.

4. *Allude* is the verb that *allusion* is derived from; *to elude* is to avoid capture or metaphorically to escape the understanding of something as in "The meaning eludes me."

5. *Principal* means "chief or main."

6. Both *gotten* and *got* are acceptable. *Gotten* is more common in American English. As a verb *loose* means "to set free" as in "Loose the dogs." Losers *lose* things and games.

7. The Sahara desert is never on the menu.

8. These two words have the same pronunciation, but *grisly* means "horrifying," and *grizzly* means "grayish or flecked with gray," which grizzly bears presumably are.

9. The metal *lead* is pronounced like the past tense of the verb *to lead*, which is *led.*

10. A *costumer* supplies costumes.

11. *Alright* is nonstandard.

12. As a verb *affect* means "to have an influence." As a noun it means a "feeling or emotion, especially as manifested by facial expression or body language." An *effect* is something brought about by a cause. As a verb *effect* means "to bring about" as in "He effected changes in procedures."

13. *Martial* is an adjective meaning "related to war or combat" as in *the martial arts. To marshal* means "to arrange or place in line for a parade, maneuver, or review." You can marshal troops or facts.

14. *Defuse* means "to remove the fuse' and by extension "to make a situation less dangerous or tense." *Diffuse* means "to pour out and cause to spread freely" or "to make less brilliant or soften."

15. *Counsel* means "advice." A *council* is an assembly of persons called together for consultation, deliberation, or discussion.

Choose the correct word:

1. When the parrot eats peanut butter, it sticks to its (palate/palette), giving it an Australian accent.

2. In his group therapy sessions, Stan tried to hide the fact that his family had not been (disfunctional/dysfunctional).

3. Sharon's propensity to cheat confined her to the (parameter/perimeter) of the mahjong club.

4. Following a strict (regime/regimen) of eating only jelly donuts, Jeremy proved his theory of the link between tastiness and weight gain.

5. When it comes to winter fashions, Edmonton is a (bellweather/bellwether) city.

6. The (baleful/baneful) look on the bouncer's face made Frank reconsider his plan to start a barroom brawl.

7. The (errant/arrant) idiocy of disconnecting the furnace became fully apparent by mid-October.

8. Cecil waited with (baited/bated) breath for an email response to his marriage proposal.

9. Wanda's voracious appetite made an (equable/equitable) sharing of the pizza unlikely.

10. Marion (flouted/flaunted) the rules of the book club and never bothered to read the books.

11. Repeated outbreaks of botulism among his customers didn't (phase/faze) Max, who continued to make hamburgers the old way.

12. We have (born/borne) the ubiquity of potholes with barely contained rage.

13. Samantha's (callous/callus) disregard for the cat's feelings seemed to please the dog.

Answers: 1. Palate **2.** Dysfunctional **3.** Perimeter **4.** Regimen **5.** Bellwether **6.** Baleful **7.** Arrant **8.** Bated **9.** Equitable **10.** Flout **11.** Faze **12.** Borne **13.** Callous

1. A *palette* is a board a painter uses to mix colours or, metaphorically, a range of colours. *Palate* means "the roof of the mouth. I'm not actually sure parrots have palates.

2. The prefix *-dys*, meaning "bad" or "difficult," comes to English from Greek language.

3. A *parameter* is a mathematical term that means "a variable which has the same value in more than one equation." A *perimeter* is the edge or border of an object and, by extension, of a group.

4. *Regime* refers to a governing body or its period of rule. A *regimen* is a system of behaviour or treatment.

5. A *bellwether* is a leader or a leading indicator of future trends. In medieval times a bell was placed around the neck of a castrated ram (a wether) to make it the leader of the flock.

6. A *baleful* look is one that menaces and foreshadows destruction. *Baneful* refers to something that is actually destructive as in "the baneful effects of a barroom brawl."

7. *Arrant* means "complete, outright, thoroughgoing. *Errant* means "wandering."

8. *Bated* from the verb bate meaning "to lessen or restrain."

9. An *equitable* distribution is a fair or just one. *Equable* means "unvarying" as in "Edmonton's equable climate" or "serene" as in "the equable attitude of Edmontonians toward winter."

10. To *flout* something is to show contempt for it. To *flaunt* something is to make an ostentatious show of it: *She flaunted her gold tooth.*

11. *Faze* is an old English verb meaning "to disconcert." As a noun, a *phase* is a stage of development; as a phrasal verb–phase in or phase out–it means to introduce or bring to an end one stage at a time.

12. *Borne* and *born* are both past participles of *bear*, but *born* is used only in passive constructions referring to birth: *I was born in Denver.*

13. Callous. *Callous* means "emotionally hardened" from the Latin *callosis*, meaning "hard-skinned."

Note: I like the Australian accent.

COMMON ERRORS

Nobody speaks in edited English, and even educated people make the occasional grammatical error. Nonetheless, one of the rewards of learning grammar is that feeling of superiority we get when we hear someone violate a grammar rule that we know. The best grammatical errors in this regard are those made by prominent persons, especially politicians and highly successful entrepreneurs (sports commentators, not so much).

See if you can find reasons to feel superior in the following utterances:

1. "In my judgment, when the United States says there will be serious consequences, and if there isn't serious consequences, it creates adverse consequences." – George W. Bush

2. For too many, to work means having less income. – Kim Campbell

3. "For Bill and I it's a real blessing." – Hillary Clinton

4. "Each of us are a part of the problem, and we need to be the solution." – Stéphane Dion

5. "If GM had kept up with technology like the computer

industry has, we would all be driving $25 cars that got 1000 MPG." – Bill Gates

6. "Having hit a wall, the next logical step is not to bang our heads against it." – Stephen Harper, Prime Minister of Canada

7. "They didn't look severely handicapped to me, I tell you. They both had cigarettes dangling from their mouth and cowboy hats." – Ralph Klein

8. "NATO needs to realize that if they continue to follow the narrow-minded agenda of the Bush administration on this issue, then they will simply fuel the cycle of violence in Afghanistan." – Jack Layton

9. "My greatest fear is the Iranians acquire a nuclear weapon and give it to a terrorist organization. And there is a real threat of them doing that." – John McCain

10. Focusing your life solely on making a buck shows a certain poverty of ambition. It asks too little of yourself. – Barack Obama

Answers:

1. Mr. Bush has a problem with subject/verb agreement. He should have said "…if there **aren't** serious consequences…" The sentence makes no sense in any case.

2. Kim Campbell used faulty parallelism. The sentence should read either "**To work** means **to have** less income, or "**Working** means **having** less income."

3. For Bill and **me**…

4. "Each of us **is** a part of the problem..." "Each" always takes a singular verb. For the sake of parallelism, we probably need to be **part** of the solution.

5. "If GM had kept up with technology **as** the computer industry has…" This is nitpicking because "like" is acceptable as a conjunction in colloquial North American English. "…we would all be driving cars that **get** 1000 MPG." Insisting on the right tense is not nitpicking.

6. "Having hit a wall" is a dangling modifier because it is followed immediately by "the next logical step," implying that the step hit the wall. A possible revision is "Having hit a wall, we should take the next logical step and not bang our heads against it."

7. Unless the unfortunates Ralph Klein was referring to had two heads and shared one mouth, they had cigarettes dangling from their **mouths.**

8. NATO is a singular noun, so it needs to realize that if **it** continues to follow…

9. Leaving "that" out in this sentence makes it awkward. It should be recast as either "My greatest fear is **that** the Iranians acquire a nuclear weapon" or "One of my greatest fears is the Iranians acquiring a nuclear weapon." There is a real threat of **their** doing that.

10. You can ask too little of yourself, but it (focusing your life solely on making a buck) asks too little of **you.**

If we required all politicians to pass a grammar test, we might have an entirely different slate of candidates.

See if you can spot the errors in the following political utterances:

1. "Canadians will see more than ever that we have the best plan for the environment, the best plan for the economy of the 21st century, for the planet and their wallet," – Stéphane Dion

2. "I am pleased to have the opportunity to reach Canadians more than ever because an election is where Canadians are focusing on the choice they have to make." – Stéphane Dion

3. "The country must have a government that can function during a time of economic uncertainty, and if it's not this government or this parliament, the public will have an opportunity to decide whom." – Stephen Harper

4. "In spite of global economic instability, Canada's economy, indeed Nova Scotia's economy, have been resilient," – Stephen Harper

5. "If you look at the tens of billions of dollars of announcements they are making, the only way these can be financed are not simply through big increases in taxes." – Stephen Harper

6. "I have only one condition for this debate, that the Prime Minister is there, because I want to debate the issues with him." – Jack Layton

7. "I found every one of those questions are the kinds of questions I'm asked at Tim Horton's." – Jack Layton

8. "I wish there was some rule against cruel and unusual punishment among campaign workers regardless of what party they belong to." – Elizabeth May

9. "There's still not enough search-and-rescue capabilities, although they're trying to fix that." – John McCain

10. "I, for one, would find it refreshing to see just one positive political ad from one of the candidates about theirselves, rather than these constant 'bash the opponent' ads." – Barack Obama

Answers:

1. Mr. Dion seems to think that Canadians share one wallet.

2. An election is not a place, so logically, Mr. Dion should have said something like "an election is a time when Canadians are focusing on the choice they have to make."

3. Whom? It's hard to see how "whom" can make sense in this sentence. Probably Mr. Harper meant that the public will have an opportunity to decide *which* government or *which* parliament.

4. Canada's economy **has** been resilient. The parenthetical "indeed Nova Scotia's economy" isn't part of the subject.

5. ...the only way these can be financed **is**... "Way" is the singular subject of the sentence.

6. Mr. Layton is no conservative and may not be interested in conserving the subjunctive, but his one condition is that the Prime Minister **be** there.

7. Every one of those questions **is the kind of question**... "Every one" is always a singular subject.

8. Since there isn't a rule against cruel and unusual punishment among campaign workers, Ms. May wishes there **were** one. It's the subjunctive again.

9. There **are** still not enough search-and-rescue capabilities. There is still not enough understanding of subject/verb agreement.

10. It may be that President Obama is trying to downplay his education, but "theirselves" exists only in non-standard dialects.

Only one of the following sentences is correct. Can you spot the errors in the others?

1. If Greta was here, she would know what to do.

2. Sara asked Dean if he were doing a gig at the club.

3. Every member will have a chance to have their voice heard.

4. Neither Colbart nor Mort have ever managed to get a date with Jadwiga.

5. We settled in for a quiet game of chess, then the idiot next door turned his stereo on full blast.

6. The upstairs toilet sprung a leak and flooded the basement.

7. Miranda flang her coat over her shoulder and marched out of the bar.

8. Bart is the best chess player in the city, and his brother is the best bridge player.

9. Nobody, not even Cecil and I, are prepared to babysit Abigail's ferret.

10. Clarence, who's skill at yodelling is legendary, was the centre of attention at the wedding reception.

11. Snodley is one of those dancing students who is always looking at his feet.

12. Like me, Geraldine gets upset when other drivers turn left.

Answers:

1. If Greta **were** here... *If* clauses that are contrary to fact require the subjunctive "were."

2. Sara asked Dean if he **was** doing a gig at the club. *If* clauses after verbs such as "ask" or "wonder" in indirect questions require the indicative "was" even if the content of the question is contrary to fact: Sara asked Dean if he was (not were) **a rabbit**.

3. The plural pronoun "their" can't refer to the singular noun "member." It used to be that the singular masculine pronoun "his" could be used here even if the members included women, but this is now considered sexist. Here are three possible revisions:

a. Every member will have a chance to have his or her voice heard.

b. All members will have a chance to have their voice heard.

c. Every member will have a chance to speak.

4. Neither Colbart nor Mort **has** ever managed... In "neither...nor" constructions, the noun closer to the verb determines whether it's singular or plural.

5. We settled in for a quiet game of chess; then the idiot next door turned his stereo on full blast. A comma can't join two independent clauses, but a semicolon can.

6. The upstairs toilet **sprang** a leak... spring, sprang, sprung. Sprung is the past participle of spring, so it would be correct to say "the upstairs toilet **has sprung** a leak."

7. Miranda **flung** her coat over her shoulder... It's sing, sang, sung, but fling, flung, flung.

8. For the sake of parallelism, we have to say where Bart's brother is the best bridge player: Bart is the best chess player in the city, and his brother is the best bridge player **in the city** (or the country, world, etc.)

9. Nobody, not even Cecil and I, **is** prepared... "Nobody" is the singular subject of the sentence.

10. Clarence, **whose** skill at yodelling is legendary... Who's is a contraction of who is.

11. Snodley is one of those dancing students who **are** always looking at **their** feet.

12. Correct.

Only one of the following sentences is correct. Can you spot the errors in the others?

1. The general consensus is that we should have a surprise party for Colbart.

2. The reason Colbart wasn't surprised was because Mort gave the secret away.

3. Abigail's elaborate plans were all for not.

4. It could of been her who called, but it didn't sound like her.

5. Mother is very upset about Aunt Edna's divorce, so be sure not to mention it around she and Pa.

6. I didn't have the heart to tell Mort that the cookies he was eating were the dogs biscuits.

7. Grating the cheese, Bart's knuckles got badly bloodied.

8. Gloria refused to tell her parents where she found the cat at.

9. The President's job approval rating has sunken lower than Edmonton's mean winter temperature.

10. Marvin thinks that you shouldn't end a sentence with a preposition. I wonder where he got that idea from?

11. Buy something healthy for dinner, i.e., fish or very lean meat.

12. Constantly searching the internet is destroying my attention… Good heavens, I have to trim my nose hairs!

Answers:

1. **The consensus** is that… The use of "general" with "consensus" is a redundancy. A consensus is general by definition.

2. "The reason was…because…" is redundant. Revised: The reason Colbart wasn't surprised was **that** Mort gave the secret away.

3. Abigail's elaborate plans were all for **naught**.

4. It could **have** been **she** who called… Rapid pronunciation of "have" misleads some to write it as "of." In formal English, the subject pronoun (I, he, she) is required after any form of the verb "to be."

5. …be sure not to mention it around **her** and Pa. The preposition "around" requires the object pronoun "her."

6. …the cookies he was eating were the **dog's** biscuits (or dogs' if there is more than one dog).

7. This is the infamous dangling modifier. The modifying phrase "Grating the cheese" has nothing it can logically modify in the rest of the sentence unless Bart's knuckles were doing the grating. **Revised:** Grating the cheese, **Bart badly bloodied his knuckles.**

8. This sentence shouldn't end with "at." This has nothing to do with the bogus rule against ending a sentence with a preposition.

It is rather the case that "at" here is unnecessary and adds nothing to the meaning.

9. The President's job approval rating has **sunk**... "Sunken" is an obsolete past participle of the verb "to sink," but it still lives as an adjective: *sunken cheeks, sunken treasure.*

10. Marvin may have got the idea from a bad source, but the question is not where he got it from, but simply where he got it.

11. Buy something healthy for dinner, **e.g.**, fish or very lean meat. The abbreviation *e.g.* means "for example."

12. Correct. The ellipsis (...) is used to represent an interruption in thought.

Of the following sentences, only three are correct. Can you spot the errors?

1. There was a moment where I thought I might win the game.

2. Everybody, including the players and the fans, were surprised by the easy victory.

3. As a teenager, politics never interested Stephen.

4. Colbart has a bad habit of barging in rooms without knocking.

5. Walking up hills frequently gives Marg leg cramps.

6. The government will give the contract to whomever makes the highest bid.

7. The new principal effected major changes in the curriculum.

8. Sedgewick takes longer breaks than anyone in the office.

9. Who is the best swimmer, Hillary or Barack?

10. Jadwiga's cat wants to eat all the time, but she feeds it only in the morning.

11. Elmo's mother who is from Nevada loves to play poker.

12. Aldo was so disinterested during the lecture that he fell asleep.

13. My being involved didn't seem to help matters.

14. Bart bought elevator shoes because he desperately wanted to be taller than me.

15. Make something light for dessert (i.e., a fruit salad or low-fat cookies).

Answers:

1. There was a moment **when** I thought I might win the game. A moment is a point in time, not place.

2. *Everybody* is the singular subject of the sentence, and the verb has to be singular: ...**was** surprised by the easy victory.

3. The phrase "As a teenager" has to be followed by someone who could have been a teenager: As a teenager, **Stephen** was never interested in politics.

4. You can walk around *in* a room, but you barge ***into*** one.

5. In this sentence "frequently" is a squinting modifier. It could be modifying either "walking" or "gives." Is it when Marg frequently walks up hills that she gets leg cramps, or does she frequently get leg cramps when she walks up hills? The sentence has to be recast to eliminate the ambiguity: *When Marg walks up hills, she frequently gets legs cramps.*

6. The government will give the contract to **whoever** makes the highest bid. One would certainly ask "To whom did the government give the bid?" But here the entire clause "whoever makes the highest bid" is the object of the preposition "to", and the subject of the clause is "whoever."

7. Correct. As a verb *effect* means to "bring about."

8. Sedgewick takes longer breaks than anyone **else** in the office. Without the "else" this sentence is illogical (sometimes grammar is logical) because Sedgewick also works in the office and would be taking longer breaks than he himself takes.

9. Who is the **better** swimmer, Hillary or Barack? When comparing two persons (or things), use the comparative form of the adjective.

10. This is a fussy point of grammar. The pronoun "she" in this sentence has no antecedent (word it can refer to). The noun "cat" obviously can't be the antecedent. But (I can hear readers objecting) surely "Jadwiga" is the antecedent. Aha, but the noun "Jadwiga" does not occur in the sentence; the possessive noun "Jadwiga's" does. A noun in the possessive can't be the antecedent of a pronoun. Few people know this, and even fewer care. The sentence has to be recast: *Although her cat wants to eat all the* *time, Jadwiga feeds it only in the morning.* Many other revisions are possible.

11. Unless Elmo has two mothers, one who is from Nevada and one who isn't, the clause "who is from Nevada" is nonrestrictive (it doesn't identify his mother) and has to be set off by commas.

12. Aldo was so uninterested during the lecture that he fell asleep. *Disinterested* means "unbiased."

13. Correct. "Me being involved..." would be wrong.

14. Correct. Some insist that only "taller than I" is correct, but respectable authorities consider "taller than me" an acceptable usage.

15. Make something light for dessert (**e.g.**, a fruit salad or low-fat cookies). The abbreviation "e.g." stands for the Latin *exempli gratia*, which means "for example." In this sentence it introduces examples of light desserts. The abbreviation "i.e." stands for the Latin *id est*, which means "that is" (literally, "it is") and is used to clarify or expand on a previous word or statement. *We skimped on dessert, i.e., we made a fruit salad.* If you can't keep these abbreviations straight, you can always use the English translations.

Of the following sentences, only one is correct. Can you spot the errors in the others?

1. When Wanda saw Murray coming, she rushed in the house to hide the whiskey.

2. Aunt Mable is reticent to speak of her years as a con artist.

3. The cat was laying on the floor next to the empty bird cage.

4. The getaway car was spotted going East on Highway 2.

5. Cedric and Chrystia can't agree on whom they think might win.

6. Ivan grew less tomatoes this year than last.

7. Snodley felt his sunburnt nose gave him a fetching look.

8. As pets, fastidious homeowners prefer hairless dogs.

9. The former vice president in charge of accounting was forced to return his bonus.

10. Sipping Campari on the French Riviera, Brad didn't feel at all bad about his role in bringing the economy down...

11. Even the prospect of sinking into abject poverty doesn't seem to effect Gloria's mood.

12. Have you seen Jack's and Martha's new house?

Answers:

1. Wanda rushed **into** the house... The preposition "in" is used for static location—Wanda is in the house—and "into" for motion to or toward.

2. Aunt Mable is **reluctant** to speak... *Reticent* means "quiet or silent." Aunt Mable may be reticent in general, but she's *reluctant* to talk about her past.

3. The cat was **lying** on the floor... *Lay* is transitive, i.e., it takes an object. You can lay the cat on the floor. I laid it there yesterday. *Lie* is intransitive, i.e., it doesn't take an object. The cat lies on the floor. I am going to lie down for a nap. One source of confusion is that the past tense of *lie* is *lay.*

4. The getaway car was spotted going **east**... The directions—north, south, west, east—are not capitalized unless they refer to a section of a country: *The South of France, the West.*

5. Cedric and Chrystia can't agree on **who** they think might win. The entire clause "who they think might win" is the object of the proposition "on." The pronoun "who" is the subject of the verb "might": who might win.

6. Ivan grew **fewer** tomatoes. Use "fewer" for things you can count; use "less" for things you can't count: less tomato juice.

7. Snodley felt **that** his sunburnt nose gave him a fetching look. The "that" can't be omitted after the verb "feel," meaning "believe" when it can be mistaken, as here, for the physical action of feeling.

8. As pets, **hairless dogs are the choice of fastidious homeowners.** If the phrase "as pets" is followed immediately by "homeowners," it implies that homeowners are pets.

9. The former vice-president... Titles such as vice-president are hyphenated outside the United States. They are capitalized only when they precede the name: American Vice President Gerry.

10. Correct.

11. Even the prospect of sinking into abject poverty doesn't seem to **affect** Gloria's mood. To affect something is to have an effect on it. As a verb, *effect* means "to bring about": Jack tried to effect changes in the office procedures.

12. Have you seen **Jack** and Martha's new house? In joint possession—Jack and Martha jointly own one house—only the second noun is in the possessive case.

Can you spot the errors in the following sentences?

1. Wanda prefers that her children are in bed by 9 p.m.

2. Abigail doesn't wear eye shadow because it makes her eyes water.

3. Check and see if I dropped my glasses in the cat's box.

4. When Uncle Harry was released from prison, he received a hardy welcome from the old gang.

5. Of the two safecrackers, Uncle Harry was by far the most skilled.

6. Anyone who gives $200 dollars or more to the campaign will receive an autographed picture of the candidate.

7. The flight attendant had smiled at Colbart, so he assumed she wouldn't object to him smoking in the rest room.

8. The amount of errors in Colbart's signed affidavit was astounding.

9. Having lived in Mexico for three years, Abigail's Spanish is excellent.

10. 200 students will enrol in Dr. Pinker's School of Clairvoyance, which will open next year.

Answers:

1. Wanda prefers that her children **be** in bed by 9 p.m. Here "be" is a subjunctive. The subjunctive form of this verb is the basic form and doesn't change for persons. The subjunctive form of the verb "to be" is "be" for all persons: I be/you be/he be/she be, etc. It is used to express commands, requests, and motions.

2. Sentences with a negative verb in the main clause followed by a dependent clause that begins with "because" are ambiguous. The sentence has to be recast to make the meaning clear. There are three possible meanings:

a. Eye shadow makes Abigail's eyes water, and that is the reason she doesn't wear it.

b. Eye shadow makes Abigail's eyes water, but that isn't the reason she doesn't wear it.

c. Abigail avoids wearing eye shadow not because it makes her eyes water (it doesn't) but for some other reason.

3. Check **to** see if I dropped my glasses in the cat's box.

4. ...he received a **hearty** welcome from the old gang. *Hardy* means "being robust or in good health." *Hearty* means "expressed warmly, exuberantly, and unrestrainedly."

5. Of the two safecrackers, Uncle Harry was by far the **more** skilled. When comparing two persons or things, use "more." Uncle Harry could be the most skilled of three safecrackers.

6. Anyone who gives $200 or more... The word "dollars" is redundant.

7. ...she wouldn't object to **his** smoking in the rest room. It's Colbart's smoking, not Colbart, that the flight attendant would object to.

8. The **number** of errors in Colbart's signed affidavit... Use "number" for things you can count and "amount" for things you can't count: the amount of sugar in Colbart's coffee.

9. Having lived in Mexico for three years, **Abigail speaks excellent Spanish**. It's Abigail, not her Spanish, that lived in Mexico for three years.

10. Two hundred students will enrol... Numbers that begin sentences are written as words. If the number is expressed in more than two words, it shouldn't begin the sentence: A total of 250 students will enrol...

Only one of the following sentences is correct. Can you spot the errors in the others?

1. If Abigail would have been there, Colbart would have tried to impress her.

2. Mort prefers Winnipeg to any city in Canada.

3. Garth gave a lecture on the nutritional value of slugs, which disgusted everybody.

4. The neurotic Mr. Snodley was both interested and repelled by cockroaches.

5. Neither of the escape plans Miranda and Sally came up with were reasonable.

6. I don't like the way that company treats their employees.

7. The exercise equipment and weights George keeps in his basement are like a gym.

8. Nobody but Jake and me really understands the psychology of ferrets in captivity.

9. Of the two grammar questions on the test, the one about comparatives was the easiest.

10. The waitress gave better service to the customers whom she believed would leave the biggest tips.

11. Jadwiga viewed a general economic collapse as a welcome distraction from her tattered love life, however, the collapse was averted.

12. A three weeks vacation were not enough to restore Sedgwick's frazzled nerves.

13. The agency requires that all requests should be submitted by July 1.

14. A recession is when you're out of work; a depression is when I'm out of work.

Answers:

1. If Abigail **had** been there… (or **Had** Abigail been there). In conditional sentences with "if clauses," the "if clause" never takes the conditional "would."

2. Mort prefers Winnipeg to any **other** city in Canada. Without the "other," it sounds as if Winnipeg isn't a city in Canada.

3. The problem in this sentence is that we don't know whether "which disgusted everybody" refers to the lecture or the fact that Garth gave it. Here is a possible revision: *Garth's lecture on the nutritional values of slugs disgusted everybody.*

4. The neurotic Mr. Snodley was both interested **in** and repelled by cockroaches. When verbs take different prepositions, both prepositions are required.

5. Neither of the escape plans Miranda and Sally came up with **was** reasonable. "Neither" is the singular subject of the sentence.

6. I don't like the way that company treats **its** employees. The plural pronoun "their" can't refer to the singular noun "company."

7. The exercise equipment and weights George keeps in his basement are like a gym's (or those in a gym).

8. Correct.

9. Of the two grammar questions on the test, the one about comparatives was the **easier**. The superlative "easiest" is used only when comparing more than two things.

10. The waitress gave better service to the customers **who** she believed would leave the biggest tips. Who = they/whom = them. She believed they (not them) would leave the biggest tips.

11. Jadwiga viewed a general economic collapse as a welcome distraction from her tattered love **life; however,** the collapse was averted. When "however" is joining two clauses, it has a semicolon before it and a comma after it. You could also write two sentences. Jadwiga viewed a general economic collapse as a welcome distraction from her tattered love life. However, the collapse was averted.

12. A three **weeks'** vacation **was** not enough to restore Sedgwick's frazzled nerves. A three weeks' vacation = a vacation of three weeks.

13. The agency requires that all requests **be** submitted by July 1. After "that" clauses that express requests or commands, the simple subjunctive "be" is required. *She asked that I be (not should be) present.*

14. Because a recession is a thing, not a time, the expression "a recession is when" is wrong, at least in formal English. The sentence is better recast:

When you're out of work, it's a recession; when I'm out of work, it's a depression.

The following sentences contain some common grammatical errors. See if you can spot them.

1. The hockey fans offered no excuse for there behaviour.

2. This winter has had it's ups and downs, mostly on the side streets.

3. If you would have waited for twenty minutes, help would have arrived.

4. Jack's apology for forgetting Valentine's Day was the most sincere I've ever heard.

5. Rachel snoring made it hard to hear the lecture.

6. I wish I was rich enough to winter in the Bahamas.

7. Daniel said he was bored of grammar because he already knew all the rules.

8. He loves being the centre of attention so much that he would only attend a funeral if he could be the corpse.

9. Neither of the pickpockets were able to identify the woman who held them up.

10. Since we've been on a diet, the dog gets way less treats.

Answers:

1. their behaviour. *Their* is the possessive pronoun.

2. its – *it's = it is.*

3. If you **had waited…** or **Had you waited…** In past conditionals like this, *would* is used only in the second part of the sentence: *If I had* (not *would have*) invested in gold, *I would be rich.*

4. sincerest. Most adjectives of one or two syllables form their comparatives and superlatives by adding the suffixes –er and –est: *sincerer, sincerest.* Adjectives of more than two syllables form their comparatives and superlatives with *more* and *most: more intelligent, most intelligent.*

5. Rachel's snoring. It was not Rachel but her snoring that made the lecture hard to hear. Such verbal forms in –ing (called "gerunds") are nouns.

6. I wish I **were** rich enough… when the clause beginning with *if* is contrary to fact, use *were.* This is called the subjunctive, and it has almost, but not quite, disappeared from English.

7. **bored with.** Daniel can be tired of grammar, but he is bored *with* it.

8. …he would attend a funeral **only** if he could be the corpse. You have to be careful to place modifiers like "only" by what they're supposed to modify.

9. Neither of the pickpockets **was** able… *Neither* is always singular and requires a singular verb.

10. The dog gets way **fewer** treats. Use less only with things you can't count: less sugar, less coffee, less dog food. Use fewer with things you can count: fewer cubes of sugar, fewer cups of coffee, fewer dog treats.

Of the following twelve sentences, only three are correct. Can you spot the errors?

1. Mildred, along with the other members of the Tai Chi club, were invited to attend the annual Tai Chi hot dog eating competition.

2. Cats often pester Bruno's dog, so he always carries pepper spray.

3. Reading often improves concentration.

4. My three brothers-in-law's ex-wives have become good friends.

5. Neither of the solutions offered were acceptable.

6. Samantha wondered why her husband was not wearing his seat belt?

7. Having tried and failed hundreds of times, Don's hopes of teaching the cat to talk began to wane.

8. Bruno had lain on the sofa for hours before he realized he was in the wrong house.

9. Of the top two students in Dr. Quack's carrot therapy class, Crystal was the best.

10. In the winter Edmonton is too cold for people to have picnics.

11. The burglars divided up the loot among themselves.

12. Earl is one of the workers who are always on time.

Answers:

1. Mildred **was** invited. The phrase "along with other members of the Tai Chi club" is not part of the subject.

2. This sentence is wrong because the pronoun "he" has no antecedent (a noun it can refer to). The antecedent can't be a possessive—*Bruno's.* The unnamed dog should be referred to as "it," but in any case, it's unlikely that the dog is carrying the pepper spray. A possible revision is "Bruno always carries pepper spray because cats often pester his dog."

3. The adverb "often" can modify either "reading" or "improving," so the sentence is ambiguous. Possible revisions: By reading often, one can improve concentration. Often concentration can be improved by reading.

4. Correct.

5. Neither of the solutions offered **was** acceptable. "Neither" is always a singular subject.

6. The sentence is a statement, not a question, so it should be punctuated with a period.

7. "Having tried and failed hundreds of times" is a dangling modifier. It wasn't Don's hopes that tried. The sentence has to be revised: "Having tried and failed hundreds of times, Don began to lose hope in the teaching the cat to talk."

8. Correct.

9. Crystal was the **better.** "Best" can be used only when comparing more than two.

10. "People" is a redundancy. In the winter Edmonton is too cold for picnics.

11. The burglars divided the loot among themselves. "Up" is redundant.

12. Correct.

Of the following twelve sentences, only three are correct. Can you spot the grammatical errors in the other nine?

1. It was she who asked his brother and him to help her sister and her push the car out of the snowbank.

2. It seems like the snow won't melt until June.

3. The streets had less potholes before the economic boom.

4. Simon, whom we thought was the best candidate, has decided not to run.

5. Edmonton's housing prices are rising faster than any city's in Canada.

6. The company offered their employees a generous benefits package.

7. Sam was in the habit of wearing his every day clothes to formal events.

8. Our mission statement is the overarching and empowering force that facilitates our realization of and commitment to the full potentialities inherent in our vision.

9. A complete list of all the items we need for the four trucks are lying on the desk.

10. Amanda is one of the teachers who stays late.

11. Gloria's science fair project, a study of the effect of low-fat cheese on depression in mice, was the most unique.

12. How has growing innumeracy impacted mail delivery?

Answers:

1. Correct.

2. It seems **as if** (or **as though**) the snow won't melt until June. In formal English, the preposition *like* can't introduce a clause.

3. The streets had **fewer** potholes before the economic boom. Use *fewer* for things you count and *less* for things you don't count: *fewer potholes, less damage.*

4. Simon, **who** we thought was the best candidate, decided not to run. *Who = he, whom = him:* We thought **he** would be the best candidate.

5. Edmonton's housing prices are rising faster than any **other** city's in Canada. Edmonton is a city in Canada.

6. The company offered **its** employees a generous benefits package. The singular noun *company* can't be the antecedent of the plural pronoun *their.*

7. Sam was in the habit of wearing his **everyday** clothes to formal events. One can do something every day, but the adjective is one word—*everyday.*

8. Correct, although meaningless. Grammar isn't everything.

9. A complete list of all the items we need for the four trucks **is** lying on the desk. *List* is the singular subject and requires the singular verb *is.*

10. Amanda is one of the teachers who **stay** late. Of the teachers who stay late, Amanda is one.

11. Gloria's science fair project, a study of the effect of low-fat cheese on depression in mice, was **unique**. *Unique*, like *pregnant* or *round*, is an absolute adjective that logically doesn't have degrees and can't be modified. Since it means "one of a kind" nothing can be more unique than something else. In popular parlance *unique* has come to mean "extraordinary" and in this sense it can be modified. One often hears "most unique," especially in advertising.

12. Correct. Many object to the use of *impact* as a verb meaning "affect," but it is a well-established usage, especially in management circles. If you don't hang out in management circles (or don't want to sound as though you do), use *affect*. The adjective "impactful" has not yet made it into most dictionaries.

Of the following sentences, only three are correct. Can you spot the errors in the other nine?

1. The childrens' books are lying on the dining room table.

2. Everybody, including the chief inspector and I, was baffled by the absence of fingerprints on the stainless steel appliances.

3. John is reticent to speak about the problem that hearing bagpipes causes him.

4. If next winter is like this winter, we're going South.

5. Everybody but me sold the stock before it collapsed.

6. Ursula rushed in the room and snatched the contaminated cat food from the cat's dish.

7. It turns out that the Mayor owns a four-wheel drive.

8. Gladys should of known that leaving the stew out overnight was a bad idea.

9. She felt bad that the guests got food poisoning.

10. It is we parents who need a break.

11. Neither of us plan to compete in the yodelling tournament.

12. If you would have come to the meetings, you wouldn't be asking why your office has been moved to the basement.

Answers:

1. The **children's** books are lying on the dining room table. The possessive of irregular plural nouns (those that don't end in *s*) are formed with an apostrophe *s* just like singular nouns.

2. Everybody, including the chief inspector and **me**, was baffled by the absence of fingerprints on the stainless steel appliances. The pronoun "me" is the object of "including."

3. John is **reluctant** to speak about the problem that hearing bagpipes causes him. *Reticent* means "quiet or silent." John may be reticent in general, but he's reluctant to speak about this particular problem.

4. If next winter is like this winter, we're going **south**. The directions—north, south, west, east—are not capitalized unless they refer to a section of a country: *The South of France, the West.* The sun sets in the west.

5. Correct.

6. Ursula rushed **into** the room and snatched the contaminated cat food from the cat's dish. Generally, "in" is used for static location—Ursula is in the room—and "into" for motion to or toward.

7. It turns out that the **mayor** owns a four-wheel drive. Titles such as mayor are capitalized only when they precede the name: Mayor Fourthright.

8. Gladys should **have** known that leaving the stew out overnight was a bad idea. "Have" is often pronounced as though it were "of," but we have to be careful to write "have."

9. Correct.

10. Correct.

11. Neither of us **plans** to compete in the yodelling tournament. Neither is a singular subject and requires a singular verb.

12. If you **had** come to the meetings, you wouldn't be asking why your office has been moved to the basement. In past conditionals, the "if" clause is in the past perfect tense.

Only three of the following twelve sentences are correct. Can you spot the errors in the nine?

1. Martha always looks like she's about to fall asleep during the grammar lecture.

2. If Gerard would have been driving the getaway car, Grandpa wouldn't be in prison today.

3. Neither Albert nor Anne has ever asked why Aunt Alice lives in the garage.

4. Jerry said to tell mother that he saw father in the bar last Sunday.

5. One-third of the class tends to be absent on the Friday before a long weekend.

6. The Russian writer, Tolstoy, had a way with words.

7. Saving globalization requires that its gains are spread more widely.

8. As an anarchist, Guilford wanted to do away with all authority so he could stay up late and eat more ice cream.

9. "Gravity," Professor Postum insisted, "Is merely a social construct."

10. The late Professor Postum subjected everyone of his theories to a rigid empirical test.

11. The flight was cancelled due to a security breach that allowed a passenger to board with toothpaste.

12. For his research paper on executions, Marvin searched the Internet for a list of famous criminals who had been hung.

Answers:

1. Martha always looks **as if** (or **as though**) she's about to fall asleep. The preposition "like" can't introduce a clause.

2. If Gerard **had** been driving… (or **Had** Gerard been driving) In such constructions, only the second clause has the conditional with "would."

3. Correct.

4. …to tell **Mother** that he saw **Father**… When kinship terms (mother, father, aunt, uncle) come before a name or take the place of a name (as in this case), they have to be capitalized.

5. Correct.

6. No commas around Tolstoy. Putting commas around Tolstoy implies that the name is not essential to the meaning of the sentence and could be dropped. "The Russian writer has a way with words." Which Russian writer? If the sentence began with Tolstoy, "the Russian writer" would be set off by commas: "Tolstoy, the Russian writer, had a way with words."

7. ...requires that its gains **be** spread more widely. A "that" clause following a verb expressing a command, request, or requirement calls for the subjunctive form *be* (not *am, is,* or *are)*: I ask that you *be* (not *are*) on time.

8. Correct.

9. "**is** merely a social construct." The word "is" should not be capitalized because it doesn't begin the quoted sentence.

10. ...**every one** of his theories... The one word "everyone" is a pronoun.

11. The flight was cancelled **because of** (or **owing to**) a security breach... *Due to* can be used only as a synonym of "caused by." One could say "The cancellation was due to (caused by) a security breach." *Due to* is so frequently used to mean "because of" that it may be approaching acceptability, but finger-wagging grammarians still object to it.

12. Marvin searched for a list of criminals who had been **hanged.** Pictures are hung, but people are hanged.

Can you spot the errors in the following sentences? One is correct.

1. If you end up going to the picnic, be sure to bring some pickles.

2. Chrystia always hides the whiskey, when Ivan is in a party mood.

3. It is absolutely essential that the candidate know Swahili.

4. Bluma told Shoshana she had won first prize.

5. We found out yesterday that Abigail won first prize.

6. The dog was much larger then I had imagined.

7. Martin has incredible executive skills, however, he declined to run for a third term.

8. When Ursula doesn't show up Theo gets depressed.
9. Let Linda or me know if you're going to be late.
10. But try and be on time.

Answers:

1. If you end up going to the picnic, be sure to **take** some pickles. Whether to use "bring" or "take" depends on the perspective of the speaker. For motion away from the speaker, use "take." For motion toward the speaker, use "bring": If you end up **coming** to the picnic, be sure to **bring** some pickles.

2. Chrystia always hides the **whiskey when** Ivan is in a party mood. No comma precedes a terminal dependent clause.

3. It is absolutely essential that the candidate **know** Swahili. Phrases such as "it is essential," indicating a demand, require the subjunctive form of the verb.

4. This sentence is ambiguous because we don't know who won first prize. It has to be recast as either "Bluma told Shoshana **that Shoshana** had won first prize" or "Bluma told Shoshana **that Bluma** had won first prize."

5. We found out yesterday Abigail **had won** first prize. Because Abigail's winning preceded our finding out about it, the past perfect tense (had won) is required.

6. The dog was much larger **than** I had imagined. For some reason "then" and "than" are often confused.

7. Martin has incredible executive **skills; however**, he declined to run for a third term. When "however" joins two independent clauses, it is preceded by a semicolon and followed by a comma.

8. When Ursula doesn't show **up, Theo** gets depressed. When a dependent clause comes before an independent clause, it must be followed by a comma. "When Ursula doesn't show up" is a dependent clause because it can't stand by itself as a sentence.

9. Correct. If you changed "me" to "I," you created a common error. If you drop "Linda or," you can see immediately that the second pronoun should be "me": "Let I know"??

10. But try **to** be on time. "Try and" is common in spoken English, but it's non-standard.

The following sentences contain grammar and punctuation errors that often appear in students' papers. Can you spot them?

1. Alexander the Great lead a very interesting life.

2. When one reads about Alexander's life, you are impressed most by his military genius.

3. He knew he was destined for greatness when he was ten years old.

4. He conquered many lands and founded alot of cities.

5. Alexander integrated many foreigners into his army, he also encouraged marriages between his soldiers and foreigners.

6. Each of Alexander's soldiers had to furnish their own footwear.

7. In 327 BC, Alexander's army marched into India, invading Punjab. As far as the river Hyphasis (modern Beas).

8. The greatest of Alexander's battles in India were the one against Porus, a powerful Indian leader.

9. When Alexander defeated Porus, he was surprised.

10. Its amazing that Alexander accomplished so much in such a short life.

Answers:

1. "Led" is the past tense of the verb "lead." The confusion probably arises from the fact that the past tense of "read" is "read," which rhymes with the metal "lead." Corrected: Alexander the Great **led** a very interesting life.

2. Shifting from one pronoun to another for no reason is an error called a pronoun shift. The most common shift in pronoun is from *one* to *you*. Corrected: When one reads about Alexander's life, **one** is impressed…

3. The clause "when he was ten years old" is misplaced in the sentence and makes it sound as if Alexander would become great at the age of ten. Corrected: When he was ten years old, Alexander knew he was destined for greatness.

4. You won't find "alot" in any dictionary, but it turns up in student papers all the time. It should be two words—*a lot*. In fact, even the correct two-word version is too informal for academic papers. Use "many" instead.

5. Here we have two sentences separated by a comma. This is a comma splice, maybe the most common punctuation error students make. Here are three ways to correct it:

a. Write two sentences: Alexander integrated many foreigners into his army. He also encouraged marriages between his soldiers and foreigners.

b. Join the two sentences with a comma and a coordinating conjunction: Alexander integrated many foreigners into his army, and he also encouraged marriages between his soldiers and foreigners.

c. Join the two sentences with a semicolon: Alexander integrated many foreigners into his army; he also encouraged marriages between his soldiers and foreigners.

6. "Each" is singular, so it requires the singular pronoun "his." Presumably, there were no women in Alexander's army. Corrected: Each of Alexander's soldiers had to furnish **his** own footwear.

7. "As far as the river Hyphasis (modern Beas)" is a sentence fragment, i.e., it has no verb or subject, but it is punctuated as if it were a sentence. Corrected: In 327 BC, Alexander's army marched into India, invading Punjab as far as the river Hyphasis (modern Beas).

8. The "greatest" refers to one battle and requires the singular verb "was." Corrected: The greatest of Alexander's battles in India **was** the one against Porus, a powerful Indian leader.

9. Who was surprised, Alexander or Porus? Here it's impossible to tell because the pronoun "he" could be referring to either of them. This is a vague pronoun reference. The only way to correct it is to get rid of the pronoun and name who was surprised: Porus was surprised when Alexander defeated him.

10. It's amazing that students still confuse "it's" (it is) with "its" (the possessive pronoun). Corrected: **It's** amazing that Alexander accomplished so much in such a short life.

The following sentences contain errors. Can you spot them?

1. I didn't bother reading *Improve Your Body Image: Make Friends Who Exercise Less Than You Do,* which was stupid.

2. Neither the Brown sisters nor Jadwiga have ever considered dating Colbart.

3. Sedgewick almost ran five miles before he remembered that the marathon had been cancelled.

4. To get ahead in life, good writing skills are a must.

5. For exercise, Carlo likes to walk his ferret or, in the winter months, he plays chess with very heavy pieces.

6. Gerald's wife, whom I believe likes to play poker, is from Nevada.

7. The chef hopes to perfect his technique for making beef taste like tofu by next Summer.

8. Samantha, who has five years experience as an animal trainer, can't get her cat to stop throwing up on the sofa.

9. Are either of the students planning to attend the workshop on subject-verb agreement?

10. Priscilla's essay was as good or better than Joan's.

11. Do you know where I can find computer accessory's?

12. The medicine had no affect on Martha's nasal congestion but it did improve her appetite.

13. Torture may not be an effective way to illicit correct answers from students.

14. Instead of standing there ringing your hands, do something.

15. Aldo is one of the workers who has never taken a vacation.

Answers:

1. What does "which" refer to? It could refer to the fact that I didn't bother to read the book or to the book itself. To eliminate this ambiguity, the sentence has to be recast: My not bothering to read *Improve Your Body Image: Make Friends Who Exercise Less Than You Do* was stupid, or I didn't bother to read *Improve Your Body Image: Make Friends Who Exercise Less Than You Do* because it is stupid. Many other revisions are possible.

2. In neither/nor constructions, the subject closer to the verb determines its number. Because the singular noun "Jadwiga" is closer, the verb must be singular: Neither the Brown sisters nor Jadwiga **has** ever considered dating Colbart.

3. "Almost" should be modifying "five miles," not "ran." Sedgewick ran ***almost*** five miles before he remembered that the marathon had been cancelled.

4. "To get ahead in life" is a dangling modifier because it isn't followed by someone who can get ahead in life (good writing skills can't get ahead). The sentence has to be recast: To get ahead in life, **one must have** good writing skills.

5. The problem here is parallelism. The two activities Carlo likes have to be expressed in parallel grammatical structures: For exercise, Carlo likes **walking** his ferret or, in the winter months, **playing** chess with very heavy pieces. For exercise, Carlo likes **to walk** his ferret or, in the winter months, **to play** chess with very heavy pieces.

6. Gerald's wife, **who** I believe likes to play poker, is from Nevada. You can decide whether to use "who" or whom" by rephrasing the clause and substituting "she" or "her": I believe *she* likes to play poker. She = who.

7. The seasons are not capitalized, so the chef hopes to perfect his technique by next **summer**.

8. Samantha has five **years'** experience as an animal trainer. *Years'* needs the apostrophe because it stands for "experience of five years."

9. Is either of the students planning… *Either* takes a singular verb.

10. Priscilla's essay was as good **as** or better than Joan's. Something can't be "as good than" something else.

11. Computer **accessories**. Apostrophes are not used to make simple plurals.

12. The medicine had no **effect** on Martha's nasal congestion, but it did improve her appetite. *Affect* is a verb that means "to have an effect." A comma before "but" is necessary. When a coordinating conjunction *(for, and, nor, but, yet, so—FANBOYS)* joins two independent clauses, it is preceded by a comma.

13. Torture may not be an effective way to **elicit** correct answers from students. *Illicit* means "unlawful." Torturing students is illicit.

14. Instead of standing there **wringing** your hands, do something (unless your hands are bells).

15. Aldo is one of the workers who **have** never taken a vacation = Of the workers who have never taken a vacation, Aldo is one.

MISPLACED and DANGLING MODIFIERS

A modifier is a word or group of words that modifies (describes or limits) another word or group of words. In the sentence, "I have a blue hat," the adjective "blue" modifies the noun "hat." In the sentence, "The man riding the camel is my cousin," the phrase "riding a camel," modifies "man." Careless writing can produce dangling and misplaced modifiers, sometimes with amusing results.

Misplaced modifiers are descriptive words, phrases, or clauses in the sentence that are not placed close enough to the words they are supposed to modify.

A dangling modifier is a word or phrase that modifies a word not clearly stated in the sentence.

What's wrong with these sentences?

1. Getting out of the car, the giant Santa became clearly visible.

2. Tripping over several shoppers at the sale, my nose was broken.

3. Lying in the gutter, I found my gift certificate.

4. Relieved of high energy costs, your Christmas lights should be bright and cheery.

5. After seeing the Christmas play, the holiday spirit filled the audience.

In each sentence the initial phrase is a dreaded **dangling modifier.** The phrases are followed by words they can't reasonably be modifying or describing.

1. The giant Santa didn't get out of the car, but somebody did. 2. My nose didn't trip over the shoppers; I did. 3. Okay, I could have been lying in the gutter when I found my gift certificate, but it's more likely that the certificate was lying in the gutter when I found it. 4. Your Christmas lights aren't relieved of high energy costs; you are. 5. Finally, the holiday spirit didn't see the Christmas play; the audience did.

The sentences must be revised:

1. Getting out of the car, **we saw the giant Santa clearly.**

2. Tripping over several shoppers, **I broke my nose.**

3. I found my gift certificate **lying in the gutter.**

4. Relieved of energy costs, **you should find your Christmas lights bright and cheery.**

5. After seeing the Christmas play, the audience was filled with the holiday spirit.

Of course, each sentence could be entirely recast:

I tripped over several shoppers and broke my nose.
We saw the giant Santa clearly once we were out of the car.

What is wrong with each of the following sentences?

1. Slipping on the ice, my glasses were broken.

2. Rachel saw a large rabbit on the way to the supermarket.

3. Expressing your thoughts clearly impressed the selection committee.

4. People who read grammar columns frequently make fewer mistakes.

5. To get ahead these days, a good education or winning a lottery is a big help.

6. Having been raised in a barn, it is difficult for him to choose the right fork.

7. Having acquired a cat, our carpet is now in shreds.

8. Our neighbour dropped by while I was cleaning the floor with an apple pie.

9. The meeting was a great success, having prepared the agenda carefully.

10. Juan only drinks three cups of coffee in the morning.

These sentences all illustrate a dangling or misplaced modifier.

Let's look at each sentence:

1. The phrase "slipping on the ice" is dangling because it has nothing to modify in the rest of the sentence. Did my glasses slip on the ice?

2. Was Rachel or the rabbit on the way to the supermarket?

3. This sentence has a misplaced modifier called a "squinting modifier." Does "clearly" modify "expressing your thoughts" or "impressed the committee"?

4. "Frequently" is another squinting modifier.

5. Who will get ahead? "To get a good education" is another dangling modifier.

6. Who was raised in a barn? "Having been raised in a barn" is a dangling modifier.

7. Did the carpet acquire the cat?

8. What do you use to clean your floor?

9. Who prepared the agenda?

10. What else does Juan do with the three cups of coffee besides drink them?

Try revising the sentences to eliminate the misplaced and dangling modifiers and compare your revisions with mine.

1. Slipping on the ice, I broke my glasses.

2. On the way to the supermarket, Rachel saw a large rabbit.

3. The clarity with which you expressed your thoughts impressed the selection committee.

4. People who frequently read grammar columns make fewer mistakes.

5. To get ahead these days, you need to get a good education or win a lottery.

6. Having been raised in a barn, he has difficulty choosing the right fork.

7. Having acquired a cat, we now have a carpet that is in shreds.

8. Our neighbour dropped by with an apple pie while I was cleaning the floor.

9. The meeting was a great success because the chair carefully prepared the agenda.

10. Juan drinks only three cups of coffee in the morning.

A reader made an interesting point about a sentence in the test that appeared in one of my columns. Readers were asked to choose the correctly punctuated sentence:

> **a.** I don't eat frogs because they make me sick.
> **b.** I don't eat frogs, because they make me sick.

The correct answer was given as ***a***. But the reader argued that ***a*** means that the fact that frogs make me sick is not the reason I don't eat them and that adding the comma would make the meaning clear. In fact, the sentence is ambiguous and should be recast:

The reason I don't eat frogs is because they make me sick or *Just because they make me sick is not the reason I don't eat frogs.* An initial negative clause followed by a *because* clause creates ambiguity. "I didn't get hired because I don't speak Albanian" could mean that my not speaking Albanian was the reason I wasn't hired. It could also mean that there was some other reason I wasn't hired, not because I don't speak Albanian.

Ambiguity in writing usually arises from placing words and phrases (modifiers) in the wrong place.

See if you can spot the ambiguity in the following sentences:

1. Anyone who cooks occasionally creates dishes that make one choke.
2. She taught a course in controlling riots at the University of Alberta.
3. We knew we would make money on the deal before it was closed.
4. Try as he might, Anthony could not explain why he wanted to get married to his cousin.
5. He eats twigs and berries only because he needs the fibre.
6. The Mayor acknowledged the role played by the police who broke up the drug ring at the annual mayoral dinner.
7. Each subscriber to a newspaper in Edmonton will receive an extra recycling box.
8. The office will issue flashlights to janitors who work in Building A and Building B.
9. We spotted the alchemist driving down the street.
10. The parishioners sponsored a paper drive to help the Katrina relief effort that they had spent months planning.

Answers:

1. Do occasional cooks create such dishes, or do all cooks occasionally create them?
2. Was the course on riots that happen at the University of Alberta or riots in general?
3. Would the money be made before the deal was closed, or did we only know about it before the deal was closed?
4. Was Anthony planning to marry his cousin or only trying to explain to her why he wanted to get married?

5. Is it only twigs and berries he eats, or does he eat them only because he needs the extra fibre?

6. Did the police break the drug ring up at the mayoral dinner or somewhere else?

7. Is it subscribing to a particular newspaper published in Edmonton or to any newspaper that merits the extra recycling box?

8. Will only janitors who work in both buildings or those who work in either building get the flashlights?

9. Were we or the alchemist driving down the street?

10. Had the parishioners spent months planning the paper drive or the Katrina relief effort?

Choose the correct sentence:

1. **a.** I read that there was an accident in the newspaper.
   b. I read in the newspaper that there was an accident.
2. **a.** He only paid the boy $3 for sweeping his walks.
   b. He paid the boy only $3 for sweeping his walks.
3. **a.** He nearly ran a quarter of a mile.
   b. He ran nearly a quarter of a mile.
4. **a.** She almost waited an hour for the rain to stop.
   b. She waited almost an hour for the rain to stop.
5. **a.** They scarcely read three chapters before falling asleep.
   b. They read scarcely three chapters before falling asleep.
6. **a.** We watched them frequently walking their dog.
   b. We frequently watched them walking their dog.

Answers: 1. b 2. b 3. b 4. b 5. b 6. b

In the exercise, only the "**b**" sentences make sense.

1. The modifying phrase *in the newspaper* is misplaced in sentence **a**, making it sound as if the accident took place in the newspaper.

2. It is clear that *only* is meant to modify the $3.

3. *Nearly* here can modify *ran* only if we mean he did something between a walk and a run for a quarter of a mile.

4. She didn't almost wait and then do something else for an hour while it rained.

5. They made it through three chapters before falling asleep, so it is clear that *scarcely* belongs directly before *three chapters.*

6. The placement of *frequently* in sentence **a** makes the meaning ambiguous. Did we watch them frequently, or were they walking their dog frequently?

The issue in these sentences is the correct placement of modifiers (words or phrases that refer to other words in a sentence). Words such as *almost, only,* and *scarcely* have to be placed directly before the words they are supposed to modify. The placement of *only*, for example, can completely change the meaning of a sentence.

Look at the placement of* only *in these sentences:

Only she can wash the car. (No one else can do it.)
She can **only** wash the car. (She can't do anything else with it)
She can wash **only** the car. (She can't wash anything else)

OLD ENGLISH

"If thou remember'st not the slightest folly
That ever love did make thee run into,
Thou hast not loved."

Shakespeare, *As You Like It.*

Some things about English are worth knowing for cultural and historical reasons. Anybody with a passing knowledge of Shakespeare or the King James Bible knows that the language has changed. We don't say *thou* or *ye* anymore, but it's a good idea to know how these words were used. A friend recently brought me the following headline for a piece in the *Globe and Mail* about giving children music lessons: "Parents: get thy children to a clarinet." It took me a minute to spot the error. *Thy* is the singular pronoun. The headline should have read "Parents: get *your* children to a clarinet." The headline writer was probably thinking of the advice Hamlet gives to Ophelia when he bids her live a life of celibacy: "Get thee to a nunnery." Had Hamlet been advising Ophelia and her sister, he would have said, "Get ye to a nunnery." So how do these archaic pronouns work?

Here is how the old pronouns differ from their modern equivalents:

Subject Forms

Singular	thou (you)
Plural	ye (you)

Object Forms

Singular	thee (you)
Plural	ye (you)

Possessive Forms

Singular	thy, thine (your)
Plural	your

My was ***mine*** and ***thy*** was ***thine*** before words beginning with a vowel: ***mine** eyes*, ***thine** eyes.*

The verbs differed a bit too. Here's the verb speak in the present tense:

I speak, thou speakest, he speaketh, we speak, ye speak, they speak.

Here are some irregular verbs:

I shall, thou shalt, he shall, we shall, ye shall, they shall
I am, thou art, he is, we are, ye are, they are

I have, thou hast, he hath, we have, ye have, they have
I do, thou dost, he doth, we do, ye do, they do.

Try substituting the old pronouns for the modern ones (change the verbs, too) in the following sentences:

1. Why don't you (singular) take your dog home?
2. Your (singular) Alaskan Husky has eaten all my apples.
3. Yes, but have you (plural) seen what your cat has done to my flowers?
4. Get your (singular) accordion and play your children a song.
5. She has no interest in cooking dinner for you (singular).

Answers:

1. Why dost thou not take thy dog home?
2. Thine Alaskan Husky hath eaten all mine apples.
3. Yes, but have ye seen what your cat hath done to my flowers?
4. Get thine accordion and play your children a song.
5. She hath no interest in cooking dinner for thee.

PUNCTUATION

Find and correct punctuation errors in the following sentences:

1. The manager asked, "How can we better incentivize staff to interface proactively"?

2. Tom asked, "Did he say, "incinerate the staff?"

3. "Oh, I hope not!", screamed Marge.

4. George said "I think "incentivize" means "encourage".

5. Alice wondered why he didn't just say he wanted to encourage us?

6. "But", I said, "it worked because now we're all interfacing."

7. "But are we interfacing proactively?", asked Bill.

8. "Let's look it up in "Merriam-Webster's Collegiate Dictionary," I suggested.

9. "Its available on line now," Tom said "So we gave the hard-copy to the local prison."

10. "We can't look it up now, Marge said, because the system is down. I'll call my cousin and ask him to look it up. He's doing time for assaulting a manager."

Answers:

1. *The manager asked, "How can we better incentivize staff to interface proactively?"* The question mark should go inside the closing quotation mark because the quotation is a question.

2. *Tom asked, "Did he say, 'incinerate the staff'?"* Quoted material within a quotation is put in single quotation marks. The question mark goes inside the double closing quotation mark because, while the manager's quotation is not a question, Tom is asking a question.

3. *"Oh, I hope not!" screamed Marge.* No comma after a quotation that ends with a question mark or an exclamation point.

4. *George said, "I think incentivize means 'encourage.'"* A comma separates a short quotation from the rest of the sentence. The word being defined is in italics, and the definition is in quotation marks. Here the definition is in single quotation marks because it is inside the quotation. Periods always go inside quotation marks.

5. *Alice wondered why he didn't just say he wanted to encourage us.* This sentence is not itself a question, but a statement, so it is punctuated with a period.

6. *"But," I said, "it worked because now we're all interfacing."* Commas always go inside the quotation marks.

7. *"But are we interfacing proactively?" asked Bill.* No comma after the quotation because it ends with a question mark.

8. *"Let's look it up in **Merriam-Webster's Collegiate Dictionary**," I suggested.* Titles of books are in italics with no quotation marks. I've added bolding here for emphasis.

9. *"It's available on line now," Tom said, "so we gave the hard-copy to the local prison."* The word "so" is not capitalized because it doesn't begin a new sentence.

10. *"We can't look it up now," Marge said, "because the system is down. I'll call my cousin and ask him to look it up. He's doing time for assaulting a manager." Marge said* is not part of the quotation.

Choose the correctly punctuated sentence:

1. **a.** We hope to visit: Paris, Rome, and Moose Jaw.

b. We hope to visit Paris, Rome, and Moose Jaw.

2. **a.** Sam claims he isn't superstitious, however, he won't take a grammar test on Friday the 13th.

b. Sam claims he isn't superstitious; however, he won't take a grammar test on Friday the 13th.

3. **a.** Joan fired three shots; then she threw the gun into the bushes.

b. Joan fired three shots, then she threw the gun into the bushes.

4. **a.** Gloria drove to the store for apples, but bought quinces instead.

b. Gloria drove to the store for apples but bought quinces instead.

5. **a.** She asked why on earth I never have enough money to pick up the tab.

b. She asked why on earth I never have enough money to pick up the tab?

6. **a.** "Why," she asked, "do you never have enough money to pick up the tab"?

b. "Why," she asked, "do you never have enough money to pick up the tab?"

7. **a.** I remembered that on Monday, March 5, 2006, I did pick up the tab.

b. I remembered that on Monday, March 5, 2006 I did pick up the tab.

8. **a.** The humorist, Woody Allen, has said that he wants to achieve immortality by not dying.

b. The humorist Woody Allen has said that he wants to achieve immortality by not dying.

9. **a.** Sigmund Freud was the father of psychoanalysis, not a designer of slips.

b. Sigmund Freud was the father of psychoanalysis not a designer of slips.

10. **a.** Submit your travel expenses and all your hotel and restaurant receipts.

b. Submit your travel expenses, and all your hotel, and restaurant receipts.

Answers:

1. **b.** The colon can introduce a list only after a complete statement. Here the colon separates the verb *visit* from its objects. One could write, "We hope to visit the following cities: Paris, Rome, and Moose Jaw."

2. **b.** When words such as *however, therefore, consequently* join two independent clauses (clauses that can stand on their own as sentences), they must be preceded by a semicolon and followed by a comma. Sometimes *however* simply interrupts the flow of a sentence and is set off with commas: *Sam, however, isn't superstitious.*

3. **a.** When a comma joins two independent clauses it's a mistake called a comma splice. Two independent clauses can be joined by a semicolon.

4. **b.** When a coordinating conjunction—*for, and, nor, but, or, yet, so (FANBOYS* is a handy acronym to remember them) joins two independent clauses, it is preceded by a comma. But here we have just one independent clause, and the conjunction *but* is joining "drove to the store" and "bought quinces instead."

5. **a.** The statement about what she asked is not a question.

6. **b.** The question mark goes inside the quotation because the quotation is a question.

7. **a.** In dates within a sentence, a comma is required after the year.

8. **b.** If one sets "Woody Allen" off with commas, it implies that the name can be left out without loss of meaning. But without the name, we would have "The humorist has said that he wants to achieve immortality by not dying." Which humorist?

9. **a.** A comma sets off contrastive elements: *not this, but that.*

10. **a.** When the coordinating conjunction *and* is joining two items (not entire clauses), no comma precedes it. If the items were listed in a series, they would be set off by commas: *Submit your travel expenses, hotel receipts, and restaurant receipts.*

Choose the correctly punctuated sentence:

1. **a.** Colbart has to have his way, otherwise, he throws a tantrum.

b. Colbart has to have his way; otherwise, he throws a tantrum.

2. **a.** We have a big problem: students are falling asleep in class.

b. We have a big problem, students are falling asleep in class.

3. **a.** Did Jadwiga ask, "Why does Colbart keep asking me for a date?"

b. Did Jadwiga ask, "Why does Colbart keep asking me for a date"?

4. **a.** Was it George W. Bush who said, "I know how hard it is for you to put food on your family."?

b. Was it George W. Bush who said, "I know how hard it is for you to put food on your family"?

5. **a.** Finding his place in the pecking order drove Cecil to drink.

b. Finding his place in the pecking order, drove Cecil to drink.

6. **a.** I'm looking for an article entitled "Material Things Do Bring Happiness" that appeared in *The Moloch Review.*

b. I'm looking for an article entitled *Material Things Do Bring Happiness* that appeared in "The Moloch Review."

7. **a.** A *slam dunk* is a basketball shot that a player makes by jumping in the air and manually powering the ball through the basket with one or both hands over the rim.

b. A "slam dunk" is a basketball shot that a player makes by jumping in the air and manually powering the ball through the basket with one or both hands.

8. **a.** In Polish "dobranoc" means *goodnight.*

b. In Polish *dobranoc* means "goodnight."

9. **a.** Garth reads philosophy all the time but doesn't understand it.

b. Garth reads philosophy all the time, but doesn't understand it.

10. **a.** When Gloria goes shopping on an empty stomach she always buys cookies.

b. When Gloria goes shopping on an empty stomach, she always buys cookies.

Answers:

1. **b.** When they join two independent clauses (clauses that can stand on their own as sentences), words and phrases such as *accordingly, consequently, curiously, furthermore, for example, however, moreover, otherwise, that is* are called "conjunctive adverbs." A semicolon comes before and a comma after the conjunctive adverb. When one of these words or phrases interrupts the flow of a single clause, it is set off by commas: *We did not, however, manage to save the sofa.*

2. **a.** A colon separates two clauses if the second clause expands on or explains the first clause. In this case, the second clause explains what the big problem is.

3. **a.** Because the quotation itself is a question, the question mark comes inside the end quotation mark.

4. **b.** The quoted sentence is a statement, not a question, so the question mark comes outside the quotation mark with no period after the statement.

5. **a.** The entire phrase "finding his place in the pecking order" is the subject of the verb "drove," so no comma comes between them. When such phrases are introductory, they are followed by a comma: *Finding his place in the pecking order, Cecil began to relax.*

6. **a.** Articles in newspapers or magazines and chapter titles in books are punctuated with quotation marks. The names of the newspapers, magazines, and books are italicized.

7. **b.** Words used with special meanings and slang terms are enclosed within quotation marks.

8. **b.** Quotation marks enclose formal definitions of words, and the words being defined are italicized.

9. **a.** The coordinating conjunctions *for, and, nor, but, or, yet, so* (FANBOYS is an acronym to help remember them) are preceded by a comma only when they are joining two independent clauses. This sentence is one clause with two verb phrases: *reads philosophy* and *doesn't understand it.*

10. **b.** When a dependent clause beginning with *when, if, after,* etc. comes first, it is followed by a comma. When a dependent clause is terminal, no comma separates it from the main clause: *Gloria always buys cookies when she goes shopping on an empty stomach.*

Choose the correctly punctuated sentence:

1. **a.** The supplies we need immediately are: paper clips, matches, and potato peelers.

b. The supplies we need immediately are paper clips, matches, and potato peelers.

2. **a.** The cities I visited are the following: Vancouver, Edmonton, and Montreal.

b. The cities I visited are the following, Vancouver, Edmonton, and Montreal.

3. **a.** Many cat owners think cats are smarter than dogs, however, evidence suggests that they just look smarter.

b. Many cat owners think cats are smarter than dogs; however, evidence suggests that they just look smarter.

4. **a.** Cats can however, be very affectionate.

b. Cats can, however, be very affectionate.

5. **a.** However, you do it, it won't work.

b. However you do it, it won't work.

Answers:

1. **b.** The colon (:) can introduce a list only after a complete sentence. No punctuation at all should come between *are* and the list.

2. **a.** *The cities I visited are the following* is a complete sentence, so the colon is required.

3. **b.** When *however* joins two independent clauses (an independent clause has a subject and a verb and makes sense), it must be punctuated with a semicolon before it and a comma after it.

4. **b.** Here *however* is not separating clauses but interrupting the flow of the sentence. It must be set off by two commas.

5. **b.** In this sentence, *however* means "in whatever way" and cannot be set off by any punctuation. Note that the comma in sentence **b** is not separating two independent clauses. *However you do it* is a dependent clause; that is, it has a subject and a verb, but it doesn't make sense on its own. When a dependent clause comes before an independent clause, it must be set off by a comma.

Apostrophe

The apostrophe is a nasty piece of punctuation mark used to show possession but is often misused. Mastering some rules for using the apostrophe will save you much embarrassment and give you many opportunities to feel superior. Here are the essential rules:

1. Never put an apostrophe before an *s* in a plural noun that ends in s: Apple's for Sale. This is known as the greengrocer's apostrophe, but you often see it in signs selling things other than vegetables and fruit: Used Car's. Never do it, and cringe when you see it. A corollary of this rule is never put an apostrophe anywhere unless you have a good reason for putting it there.

2. One good reason for putting an apostrophe in is to take the place of a missing letter or letters in a contraction. Note the following contractions: it's (it is), we're (we are), you're (you are).

3. Another good reason for slipping in an apostrophe is to make a noun possessive. Let's say your aunt has left her pen on the table. You can say, "The pen of my aunt is on the table." But this sentence sounds a bit like French. The normal way of saying this in English is to make aunt possessive by putting an apostrophe *s* on the end: "My aunt's pen is on the table." The words "my aunt's pen" = "the pen of my aunt." Any singular noun can be made possessive this way: the dog's left leg, Jadwiga's sleeping pills, Prime Minister Harper's smile. But what about plural nouns? See the next paragraph.

4. Make plural nouns that end in *s* possessive by putting an apostrophe after the *s*: "My two aunts' pens are lying on the table." Any plural noun that ends in *s* can be made possessive this way: the gangsters' guns, the hypochondriacs' fatal illnesses, the attorneys' briefs. But what about plural nouns that don't end in *s*? See the next bullet.

5. Make plural nouns that don't end in *s* possessive by putting an apostrophe *s* on the end just as you do for singular nouns: the oxen's supper, the women's glass ceiling, the children's Rottweilers.

6. Compound nouns like brother-in-law make just the principal noun plural: brothers-in-law. Both the singular and the plural possessives of such nouns are made with an apostrophe *s* after the final word: my brother-in-law's wife; my brothers-in-law's wives. (Of course it's simpler to say my sisters-in-law).

7. For the singular possessive of names that end in an *s* sound, you have a choice. You can write either "Mr. Jones' car" or "Mr. Jones's car." The plural possessive of such nouns is regular: the Joneses' house.

8. For nouns that jointly possess something, only the second noun is possessive: Jack and Jill's diner (The diner belongs to both of them). Jack's and Jill's haircuts (They don't share one haircut).

9. Sometimes the thing "possessed" is understood: Moira's cat is fatter than Cecil's. The meaning changes considerably if you don't make Cecil possessive.

10. Names of companies that already have an apostrophe don't take another apostrophe for the possessive: MacDonald's hamburgers (not Macdonald's' hamburgers.)

11. Periods of time can have a possessive construction: one week's vacation = a vacation of one week; two weeks' vacation = a vacation of two weeks.

12. Here's the really confusing part: The possessive pronouns—hers, its, ours, yours, theirs—don't have apostrophes.

Widespread confusion about the apostrophe has prompted the founding ofThe Apostrophe Protection Society, a UK organization that may well have adherents around the world.

Choose the correct words:

1. My (father's and mother's/father and mother's) car was stolen last night.

2. Dad said (its/it's) a good thing because the car was a gas-guzzler.

3. The (Smith's/Smiths) hope (their's/theirs) is stolen, too.

4. Dad went to buy Mom some good walking shoes, but he couldn't find the (womens'/women's) department.

5. The dog buried (it's/its) bone in the (Johnson's/Johnsons') yard.

Answers: 1. father and mother's **2.** it's **3.** Smiths, theirs **4.** women's **5.** its, Johnsons'

1. The *'s* should be deleted from *father*. For joint possession—they both own the car—only the second noun is in the possessive. But—*my father's and mother's signatures.*

2. Dad is saying that *it is a good thing. It's* is the contraction of *it is.*

3. The plural of the family name *Smith* is simply *Smiths* with no apostrophe. *Their's* should be *theirs* without the apostrophe. Possessive pronouns—*his, hers, its, yours, ours, theirs* never take apostrophes.

4. The possessive of *women* is *women's*. Irregular plural nouns that don't end in *s (women, children*, etc.) form their possessive with *'s* just like singular nouns.

5. No apostrophe in possessive pronouns, so *its bone.* Regular plural nouns that end in *s* have the apostrophe after the *s* in the possessive. *The Smiths' car.* The yard belongs to the Johnsons, so *the Johnsons' yard.*

Try the following quiz. Add an apostrophe or an apostrophe s where appropriate and correct contractions. The following sentences are for practice with apostrophes and are not models of good style:

1. Both parents children have three weeks allowance coming.

2. My two brothers five friends dogs are staying at my Nephew Barrys parents house.

3. Your going to be very surprised at the Liberals nominee.
4. The CEO got five years pay for an honest days work.
5. My aunt and uncles camel died.
6. Mr. Lopez father and mothers signatures are indistinguishable.
7. This years prices for smoked eel are much higher than last year.
8. After lunch were all going over to the Smiths.
9. Wendy's hamburgers taste best hot.
10. Janes sisters-in-laws cooks cooking is better than hers or her own cooks.

Answers: 1. parents', weeks' **2.** brothers', friends', Barry's, parents' **3.** you're, Liberals' **4.** years', day's **5.** uncle's **6.** Lopez' or Lopez's, father's, mother's (They each have a signature). **7.** This year's, last year's [prices] **8.** we're, Smiths' [house] **9.** No additional apostrophe **10.** Jane's, sisters-in-law's, cooks', cook's (assuming that the sisters-in-law have one cook each, and Jane has just one cook.)

Rewrite the following phrases to show possession using an apostrophe:

1. the work of the committees
2. the house of the Murphys
3. the cars belonging to the companies
4. the hardhats of the construction workers
5. the smoking jackets belonging to the men
6. the car my brother and sister-in-law bought
7. the novels of Steinbeck and Hemmingway
8. the law firm of Pinkerton and Kowalski
9. the work of a single month
10. the bonuses of the CEOs
11. the game plans of both teams
12. the inheritances of their offspring
13. the salary of four months
14. the meeting of last Wednesday
15. the classes of next year

Answers: 1. the committees' work **2.** The Murphys' house **3.** the companies' cars **4.** the construction workers' hardhats **5.** the men's smoking jackets **6.** my brother and sister-in-law's car **7.** Steinbeck's and Hemmingway's novels **8.** Pinkerton and Kowalski's law firm **9.** a single month's work **10.** the CEOs' bonuses **11.** both teams' game plans **12.** their offspring's inheritance **13.** four months' salary **14.** last Wednesday's meeting **15.** next year's classes

Commas and Semicolons

Most errors in punctuation are comma errors. By mastering some rules and some grammatical concepts, one can eliminate comma errors and feel more confident about writing. Let's look at the rules for punctuating complex sentences. A complex sentence consists of one **independent clause** and one **dependent clause**. An **independent clause** has a subject and a verb and makes sense by itself.

***Here's an example of an* independent clause:**

He always gets sick.

He is the subject, and *gets* is the verb. Note that I can end this clause with a period because it is a sentence. A **dependent clause** has a subject and a verb, but it doesn't make sense by itself.

***Here's an example of a* dependent clause:**

Whenever he eats too much pizza…

He is the subject, and *eats* is the verb, but I can't put a period at the end of this clause because it doesn't make sense. It isn't a sentence by itself. *Whenever he eats too much pizza…* what? We can combine these two clauses into one complex sentence.

Here are two comma rules:

Rule One: If the **dependent clause** comes first, put a comma after it:

Whenever he eats too much pizza, he gets sick.

Rule Two: If the **independent clause** comes first, don't put a comma after it:

He gets sick whenever he eats too much pizza.

Here are some words that introduce dependent clauses:

after, although, as, because, if, whether, though, since, even, unless.

Identify the words in bold type as either an independent or a dependent clause and punctuate the sentence:

1. **If oil revenues stay high** we'll all be rich.
2. **Take a few minutes to think** before you answer.
3. I had to take the bus **after the car had a flat.**
4. When the topic turns to commas **I always fall asleep**.
5. **Because we love opera** we always buy season tickets.
6. **Although we worry about global warming** we love warm winters.

Answers: 1. dependent (comma after *high*) **2.** independent (no comma) **3.** dependent (no comma) **4.** independent (comma after *commas*) **5.** dependent (comma after *opera*) **6.** dependent (comma after *warming*)

Commas or Semicolons

Deciding whether to use a comma or a semicolon can be very stressful. You can reduce the stress by learning how to punctuate compound sentences and series.

Look at these sentences:

Colbart hates grammar.
He often skips grammar class.

Both are independent clauses. They're called independent clauses because they can stand on their own as sentences. Note that a clause has to have at least one subject and one verb. In the first sentence, the subject is *Colbart,* and the verb is *hates*. In the second sentence, the subject is *he,* and the verb is *skips*.

One independent clause is a **simple sentence**. Two simple sentences can be joined by a coordinating conjunction (*for, and, nor, but, or, yet, so*—FANBOYS is a handy acronym) to make one **compound sentence.**

A comma comes before the coordinating conjunction:

Colbart hates grammar, and he often skips grammar class.

Take out the subject "he" in second clause, and the comma before "and" comes out too. The compound sentence becomes a simple sentence with one subject (Colbart) and two verbs (hates and skips).

Colbart hates grammar and often skips grammar class.

Two independent clauses can (almost) NEVER be joined by just a comma. This is an error called a *comma splice.*

Colbart hates grammar, he often skips grammar class.

Very short, pithy clauses can be joined by a comma:

Man plans, God laughs.

BUT two independent clauses CAN be joined by a semicolon to form a compound sentence. Two clauses joined by a semicolon must be closely related thoughts that belong together.

Colbart hates grammar; he often skips grammar class.

The following are clearly not closely related thoughts:

Colbart hates grammar; his sister is very tall.

Three or more items in a series are separated by commas:

Attending the meeting were Bob Windbag, Sara Soporific, and Dan Gobbledygook.

BUT if the series itself contains commas, the items are separated by semicolons:

Attending the meeting were: Bob Windbag, Administration; Sara Soporific, Human Resources; and Dan Gobbledygook, Mission Statement Facilitation.

Transitional words and phrases (sometimes called *conjunctive adverbs*) such as *accordingly, consequently, curiously, furthermore, for example, however, moreover* can join two independent clauses.

When one of these words or phrases joins two independent clauses, a semicolon comes before it and a comma after it:

Colbart hates grammar; consequently, he often skips grammar class.

When one of these transitional words or phrases interrupts the flow of a single clause, it is set off by commas:

Colbart, however, loves math.

Punctuate the following sentences with commas or semicolons as appropriate and decide whether each sentence is a simple sentence (one clause) or a compound sentence (two clauses):

1. Bart and his friends often drink too much and get sick.
2. Priscilla gets very involved in chess problems sometimes she forgets to eat.

3. Don had no coffee beans in his flamed Sambuca and Linda had four in hers.

4. Doug and Evie took the coffee beans out of their flamed Sambuca and offered them to Don.

5. We just met Sam Joe's father Marion Sam's second wife and Cleo and Eleanor their two Siamese cats.

6. Ursula and Theo love taking long walks together however Theo is getting old and can't walk very far anymore.

7. Martin will try to get out of running for a third term but the board won't let him.

8. Geraldine never worries about being late she is however rarely late for dinner.

9. Cedric loves dogs but has never owned one.

10. Cedric loves dogs however he has never owned one.

Answers:

1. No commas or semicolons (simple)

2. Priscilla gets very involved in chess problems; sometimes she forgets to eat. (compound)

3. Don had no coffee beans in his flamed Sambuca, and Linda had four in hers. (compound)

4. No commas or semicolons (simple)

5. We just met Sam, Joe's father; Marion, Sam's second wife; and Cleo and Eleanor, their two Siamese cats. (simple)

6. Ursula and Theo love taking long walks together; however, Theo is getting old and can't walk very far anymore. (compound)

7. Martin will try to get out of running for a third term, but the board won't let him. (compound)

8. Geraldine never worries about being late; she is, however, rarely late for dinner. (compound)

9. No commas or semicolons (simple)

10. Cedric loves dogs; however, he has never owned one. (compound sentence)

Put commas or semicolons where appropriate in the following sentences:

1. Gloria worked as a waitress for many years and now she owns a pizzeria.

2. The dog's owners claim it's a genius but the dog flunked obedience school.

3. The dog thought it was going to the vet to be "tutored" the cat knew the truth.

4. We plan to visit London Paris and Rome.

5. Cat owners always think their cats are smart however I have never seen a cat that knows its name.

6. We plan to visit London England Paris France and Rome Italy.

7. Sara's pet frog had a short happy life.

8. We would prefer however to spend some time in Mexico before we make our final decision.

9. We want to retire in Mexico therefore we plan to study Spanish.

10. Juanita ordered a huge carrot muffin.

Answers:

1. Gloria worked as a waitress for many years, and now she owns a pizzeria.

2. The dog's owners claim it's a genius, but the dog flunked obedience school.

3. The dog thought it was going to the vet to be "tutored"; the cat knew the truth.

4. We plan to visit London, Paris, and Rome.

5. Cat owners always think their cats are smart; however, I have never seen a cat that knows its name.

6. We plan to visit London, England; Paris, France; and Rome, Italy.

7. Sara's pet frog had a short, happy life.

8. We would prefer, however, to spend some time in Mexico before we make our final decision.

9. We want to retire in Mexico; therefore, we plan to study Spanish.

10. Juanita ordered a huge carrot muffin.

The first three sentences are compound sentences, meaning that each consists of two independent clauses. Remember that an independent clause has a subject and a verb and makes sense by itself. The two independent clauses in the **first sentence** could be separate sentences: *Gloria worked as a waitress. Now she owns a pizzeria.* Two independent clauses can be combined into one compound sentence in two ways. They can be joined by a coordinating conjunctions—*for, and, nor, but, or, yet, so* (FANBOYS).

When a coordinating conjunction joins two independent clauses, a comma must precede the conjunction: *Gloria worked as a waitress, and now she owns a pizzeria.* They can also be joined by a semicolon without a conjunction as in **sentence 3:** *The dog thought it was going to the vet to be "tutored"; the cat knew the truth.* Two independent clauses can **never** be joined by just a comma. This is an error called a **comma splice.**

Sentences 4 and 5 each contain a series or list. Normally, three or more items in a series are separated by commas. A comma before the *and* is optional, but most punctuation styles include it. **In sentence 5**, each item in the list contains a comma, so to avoid a confusing profusion of commas, the items are separated by semicolons.

Sentences 6 and 7 have independent clauses joined by the conjunctive adverbs *however* and *therefore*. These words are always set off by a semicolon and a comma when they join independent clauses. Note that these could also be written as separate sentences. **In sentence 8**, *however* is not joining two clauses and is simply set off by commas. **In sentence 9**, the two adjectives *short* and *happy* are coordinate adjectives and must be separated by a comma. Adjectives are coordinate when they can be reversed and still make sense: a short, happy life or a happy, short life. **In sentence 10**, the adjectives *huge* and *carrot* are not coordinate, so no comma comes between them. A carrot huge muffin?

In editing it's a good idea to look at every coordinating conjunction and decide what stands on either side of it. If it joins two independent clauses or the final item in a list, put a comma before it. If it joins anything else, don't put the comma: *We went to the store, and we bought bread. We went to the store and bought bread.* The phrase *bought bread* is not an independent clause because it lacks a subject. Here the *and* is joining the two verbs *went* and *bought*, so no comma precedes it.

Choose the correctly punctuated sentence:

1. **a.** We underestimated the cost of the project, consequently, we went over budget.

   b. We underestimated the cost of the project; consequently, we went over budget.

2. **a.** Who said, "I don't want to achieve immortality through my work; I want to achieve it through not dying?"

   b. Who said, "I don't want to achieve immortality through my work; I want to achieve it through not dying"?

3. **a.** Showing up on time, staying awake at work, and appearing to listen – these are the life skills the course will cover.

   b. Showing up on time, staying awake at work, and appearing to listen: these are the skills the course will cover.

4. **a.** We have a big problem, students are falling asleep in class.

   b. We have a big problem: students are falling asleep in class.

5. **a.** The biggest problem facing writers, namely, having something to say, never seems to bother politicians.

   b. The biggest problem facing writers—namely, having something to say—never seems to bother politicians.

6. **a.** Please bring the following to the first class:

   1. A box of crayons
   2. Two paper cups
   3. Three dead goldfish

   b. Please bring the following to the first class:

   1. A box of crayons;
   2. Two paper cups;
   3. Three dead goldfish.

Answers: 1. b 2. b 3. a 4. b 5. b 6. a

Choose the correctly punctuated sentence:

1. **a.** Bart cooks slugs to perfection, however, his ingrate kids refuse to eat them.

b. Bart cooks slugs to perfection; however, his ingrate kids refuse to eat them.

2. **a.** We have a big problem: Grandpa has squirrels living in the attic.

b. We have a big problem, Grandpa has squirrels living in the attic.

3. **a.** Who asked, "Do you find it unnerving that doctors call what they do 'practice'?"

b. Who asked, "Do you find it unnerving that doctors call what they do 'practice?'"

4. **a.** Who said, "My parents were so cheap that they used to take me to the pet store and tell me it was the zoo"?

b. Who said, "My parents were so cheap that they used to take me to the pet store and tell me it was the zoo."?

5. **a.** Forgoing showers for several days, provided Cecil with the personal space he craved.

b. Forgoing showers for several days provided Cecil with the personal space he craved.

6. **a.** There was a very interesting article entitled *Oil Companies Forgo Profits to Lower Prices* in last Sunday's "Fantasy Times" newspaper.

b. There was a very interesting article entitled "Oil Companies Forgo Profits to Lower Prices" in last Sunday's *Fantasy Times* newspaper.

7. **a.** In Edmonton a *no scratcher* is a summer day relatively free of mosquitoes.

b. In Edmonton a "no scratcher" is a summer day relatively free of mosquitoes.

8. **a.** The Latin word "sic" means *thus* or *so*, not *spelling is correct.*

b. The Latin word *sic* means "thus" or "so," not "spelling is correct."

9. **a.** Garth went to the store but forgot to buy Plantains.

b. Garth went to the store, but forgot to buy Plantains.

10. **a.** Garth's wife Grace went to the store, and she remembered to buy Plantains.

b. Garth's wife Grace went to the store and she remembered to buy Plantains.

Answers: 1. b 2. a 3. b 4. a 5. b 6. b 7. b 8. b 9. a 10. a

1. When *however* joins two independent clauses, it is punctuated with a comma before it and a semicolon after it. Independent clauses can stand on their own as sentences. *Bart cooks slugs to perfection. His ingrate kids refuse to eat them.*

2. A colon can separate two independent clauses if the second clause explains or expands on the first clause. Here the second clause explains what our problem is.

3. A quotation that appears within another quotation has single quotes. If the quoted material is a question, the question mark goes inside the quotation marks, including single quotation marks.

4. If the sentence is a question, but the quoted material within the statement is not a question, the question mark goes outside the quotation marks.

5. The phrase "Forgoing showers for several days" is the subject of the sentence and cannot be separated from the verb by a comma. If the phrase were introductory, it would be set off by a comma: *Forgoing showers for several days, Cecil stank to high heaven.*

6. Articles in newspapers or magazines and chapter titles in books are punctuated with quotation marks. The names of the newspapers, magazines, and books are italicized.

7. Words used with special meanings and slang terms are enclosed within quotation marks.

8. Quotation marks enclose formal definitions of words, and the words being defined are italicized.

9. The coordinating conjunctions *for, and, nor, but, or, yet, so* (FANBOYS is an acronym to help remember them) are preceded by a comma only when they are joining two independent clauses. This sentence is one clause with two verb phrases: *went to the store and forgot to buy.*

10. Here the comma is required because "and" is joining two independent clauses that can stand as sentences on their own: *Garth's wife Grace went to the store. She remembered to buy Plantains.*

Hyphens

Rules for using hyphens are complicated, and anybody who has to do a lot of writing should have a good reference manual handy. Here are some useful guidelines:

1. Compound adjectives are generally hyphenated when they come before a noun: *a gas-guzzler car, a four-story building, a five-year-old child.*

2. Compound adjectives are generally not hyphenated when they follow a noun: *the car is a gas guzzler, the building is four stories, the child is five years old.*

3. Some compound adjectives are always hyphenated whether they come before or after a noun. Such permanently hyphenated compound adjectives will appear as hyphenated in an up-to-date dictionary (or in a dictionary that is up to date): *short-term, part-time.*

4. Combinations of adverbs that end in –ly and adjectives are never hyphenated: *purely selfish motives, completely absurd ideas.*

5. Combinations of adverbs that don't end in –ly and adjectives are hyphenated when they come before a noun: *her long-awaited arrival* (but *Her arrival was long awaited.*) Comparatives and superlatives—*more, most, better, best, less least*—are not hyphenated: *the best laid plans, the most egregious errors.* Compound adjectives in which the second element is a number are not hyphenated: *a grade 3 student.*

6. The current trend is not to hyphenate words prefixed by *non, un, in, dis, co, anti, hyper, pre, re, post, out, bi, counter, de, semi, mis, mega, micro, multi, inter, over, under.* For example: *nonaffiliated, nonemergency, uninfected, inpatient, disorder, disbar, coworker.* But there are many exceptions. If the prefixed word begins with the same letter that the prefix ends in or is capitalized, it is hyphenated: *anti-intellectual, un-Canadian.* Double *e's* and double *o's* are usually made into one word: *reenter, coordinate.*

The prefixes *self, all,* and *ex* almost always require a hyphen: *ex-wife, self-confident, all-knowing.* Hyphens are also used with prefixes to avoid confusion: for example, *re-count* meaning "to count again" is hyphenated to distinguish it from *recount* meaning "to tell." A hyphen is used to avoid the occurrence of three letters together: *bell-like.*

7. Recent two-word technological terms have tended to evolve into single words (closed compounds.) For example, *email, online,* and *database* are replacing earlier two-word or hyphenated forms.

8. Frequently used compound nouns such as *data processing, home office, car insurance* are not hyphenated when they are used as adjectives: *a car insurance policy, the data processing department.*

When in doubt always check a current dictionary or reference manual.

Choose the correct form:

1. The play was a (low-budget/low budget) production.

2. The Prime Minister is (well-known/well known) for his fashion sense.

3. Unfortunately the repair was (out-of-warranty/out of warranty) by the time it was done.

4. The plan for Iraq has to be (fine-tuned/fine tuned) fairly soon.

5. Even a (carefully-planned/carefully planned war) can go awry.

6. The gangster was a (friendly-looking/friendly looking) fellow.

7. Please (re-submit/resubmit) your application with details of the "extensive" experience you've had.

8. Conrad owns a (filthy-magazine/filthy magazine) store in Moose Jaw.

9. You'll have to (re-sort/resort) these cards.

10. We bought a (better-built/better built) mousetrap.

11. Amanda was diagnosed with (Type-2/Type 2) diabetes.

12. Why is the (checkout/check-out) line always flanked by magazines featuring diet plans on one side and candy bars on the other?

13. It takes a lot of work to become a (first-class/first class) chess player.

14. I found an interesting (web-site/website) devoted to debunking astrology.

15. After completing a PhD in philosophy, she became a (real-estate/real estate) agent.

Answers: **1.** low-budget **2.** well-known **3.** out of warranty (Before the noun, it would be hyphenated: an out-of-warranty repair.) **4.** fine-tuned (Although one encounters *fine tuned*, dictionaries give *fine-tuned.*) **5.** carefully planned **6.** Friendly-looking (Here *friendly* is an adjective.) **7.** resubmit **8.** Either could be correct, depending on the meaning (If Conrad owns a store that sells filthy magazines, the hyphen serves to distinguish it from a magazine store that happens to be filthy.) **9.** re-sort (*Resort* has another meaning.) **10.** better built. **11.** Type 2 **12.** checkout **13.** first-class (As an adjective *first-class* is always hyphenated. As a noun, it isn't hyphenated: *He was of the first class.*) **14.** website (Originally, *Web site* was more common.) **15.** real estate

CAPITALIZATION

Capitalize words where required in the following sentences:

1. After repeatedly flunking physical education, Garth decided to major in greek.

2. Once Shawn passes anthropology 603, he will have finished the course work for his master's degree.

3. James saw that the package was marked "fragile" only after he dropped it.

4. My mother grew up in the west, but father was an easterner.

5. Is a polytheist a worshipper of many gods or a toothpaste?

6. "You really should try," uncle Bart said, "not to feed the dog asparagus."

7. The dog, a Chihuahua-retriever cross, likes to hunt but hates winter.

8. The wedding gifts included a teflon frying pan, and a kodak camera.

9. To save money, the Smiths decided to serve the champaign for the wedding reception in styrofoam cups.

10. From a darwinist perspective, the vice-president was not a great success.

11. Mrs. Snodlebridge always closed her letters "devotedly yours."
12. Harold soon discovered that giving the prices for his gourmet french fries in roman numerals only confused his customers.

Answers:

1. **Greek** – Since physical education is not the name of a specific course, it is not capitalized. Greek is capitalized because the names of languages are always capitalized. *I took math, geology and Spanish.*

2. **Anthropology** – Specific courses are capitalized. General references to academic degrees are not capitalized. Abbreviations of degrees are: *Shawn has an M.A.*

3. **Fragile** – Words that follow the words *marked* or *stamped* are capitalized. Capitalize only the first word in a phrase: *My vet bill was marked "Paid in full."*

4. **West, Father** – Points on the compass are capitalized when they refer to specific regions. When kinship terms (my mother, your father, his aunt) are used with the possessives, they are not capitalized. But they are capitalized when they precede names (Aunt Jane) or when they are used instead of names (Where is Father?).

5. We don't capitalize the word "god" unless it refers specifically to God. If you're an atheist and want to always write "god," be sure to find an editor who is also an atheist.

6. **Uncle** (See the answer for sentence 4.)

7. **Chihuahua-retriever** – Proper names and place names describing dog breeds are capitalized but not the generic type of dog, thus Labrador retriever/golden retriever, King George spaniel/springer spaniel, and Rottweiler (because the breed is associated with a German city called Rottweil). If you happen to be writing for a kennel club, capitalize the complete names of all dog breeds. Note that seasons are not capitalized, so *winter* remains in lower case.

8. **Teflon, Kodak** – Brand names that are protected by trademark laws are always capitalized, but note that the generic name of the product following a brand name is not capitalized. Lists of protected trademark names can be found on the Internet.

9. Champaign, Styrofoam – These are both proper nouns.

10. Darwinist – Adjectives derived from proper names are capitalized: Newtonian physics, Keynesian economics.

11. Devotedly yours – In formal letter closings, only the first word is capitalized.

12. French, Roman – Not all dictionaries agree that the "French" in French fries is capitalized.

9. Champaign, [illegible]: [illegible] both proper [illegible]

10. Darwinian: Adjectives derived from proper nouns [illegible] Newtonian [illegible]

11. [illegible] changes only [illegible] [illegible].

12. [illegible] agree [illegible] [illegible].

PET PEEVES

When I began writing my "Grammar Gaffes" column in 2007, readers often sent me grammatical pet peeves that made them cringe, cry, and sometimes—as one reader put it—"want to slap somebody silly" (the Tony Soprano approach to language instruction.)

Here is a potpourri of "best" pet peeves that readers have urged me to mention. Be warned that some of these are pretty shocking. You might want to keep this section of the book away from your children.

Policing grammar is a hard job. *Nil desperandum.* (Is using foreign phrases anyone's pet peeve?)

1. Using *hopefully* to mean "it is hoped" or "I hope" as in "Hopefully, the burglars will be caught." Some grammarians and others argue that this usage is incorrect because *hopefully* means "full of hope" and doesn't make sense when used this way. Will the burglars be full of hope when they are caught? Other grammarians—probably a majority—argue that *hopefully* is a sentence adverb and is perfectly acceptable. Some other sentence adverbs are *fortunately, happily,* and *sadly*. Few would object to

"Fortunately, the burglars were caught." If you use *hopefully* in the sense of "it is hoped," be aware that some will think you're making an error. On the other hand, some actual errors are so widespread that if you don't make them, many will think you are making an error.

2. Confusing *lie* and *lay.* I have devoted an entire column to the difference between these two verbs. Here are examples of their correct use: *lie—Today I lie on the sofa. Yesterday I lay on the sofa. I have lain on the sofa for hours. Lay—Today I lay the cat on the sofa. Yesterday I laid the cat on the sofa. I have repeatedly laid the cat on the sofa.*

3. Mispronouncing *etc. (et cetera)* as *ex cetera.* This is a very common mispronunciation, which is not surprising considering that these days even scholars don't necessarily know much Latin. Determine whether you have a tendency to make this mispronunciation, and if you do, say "and so forth" instead.

4. Confusing the abbreviations e.g. and i.e. More Latin! The abbreviation e.g. stands for the Latin *exempli gratia*, which means "for example." Here's an example of how it is used: "John always bought his wife expensive gifts, e.g., a diamond necklace and a purebred Irish Wolfhound." The abbreviation i.e. stands for the Latin *id est*, which means "that is" (literally, "it is") and is used to clarify or expand on a previous word or statement. "John's wife disposed of one gift, i.e., she poisoned the Irish wolfhound." If you can't keep these abbreviations straight, you can always use the English translations.

5. Using *literally* to mean "figuratively" as in "The dog literally ate us out of house and home." *Literally*, which means "exactly as described; in a literal way" (or literally, "by the letter") has long been used as a simple intensifier of statements that are already exaggerations. I suspect *literally* is being overused, and it's the overuse that is causing consternation.

6. Using the wordy expression "at this point in time" for "now." This drives me crazy, too. The same people who have turned this phrase into a grating cliché have recently been replacing "finally" with "at the end of the day." All we can do is roll our eyes.

7. Using *orientate* for "orient" as in "He stood for a minute to orientate himself in the new surroundings." *Orientate* is a verb formed from the noun *orientation* by removing the suffix –tion. This is called a back-formation. Some other back-formations are *adulate* from *adulation, babysit* from *babysitter,* and *greed* from *greedy* (originally the noun was *greediness).* The formation of new words in this way is a normal process, although it takes time for a back-formation to become accepted. By now *orientate* is an acceptable variant of *orient*, but it's more common in the British English.

8. Confusing *farther* and *further.* Some authorities consider these adverbs interchangeable except that only *further* can mean "moreover" or "in addition to": "Harold stated further that he was too busy to attend the meeting." Others reserve *farther* for actual physical distance—*How much farther do we have to travel*—and further for metaphorical distance—*How much further can we belabour this issue?*

9. Using the redundant "why" as in "The reason why Colbart became a fitness instructor is increasingly unclear." This usage has been denounced by some authorities and defended by others. One usage manual points out that reputable writers have used this construction since the Renaissance. I prefer to avoid it, although I don't always succeed.

10. Saying *the exact same*, as in "You keep making the exact same error." This is acceptable colloquial usage, but it sounds wrong to anybody with a passing knowledge of adverbs. It should be *exactly the same.*

11. Saying *bored of,* as in "I'm bored of having my grammar corrected." I first noticed this usage many years ago when my kids started saying it (I never slapped them). One says *sick of* or *tired of* or *sick and tired of,* but not **bored of.** It should be ***bored with.***

12. Saying *one of the only*, as in "She's one of the only women I know who eats slugs." As an adjective, *only* always refers to just one thing or person—*an only child, the only one*—and can't logically modify the plural *women.* The sentence should read, "She's one of the **few** women I know who eats slugs." In fact, of course, she's probably the only woman who eats slugs.

13. Confusing *its* and *it's*, as in "Its a shame that the cat broke it's tail." Remember that *its* is the possessive pronoun, and *it's* is a contraction of "it is." The sentence should be "It's a shame that the cat broke its tail."

Also, using an apostrophe in simple plurals (this is known as the *greengrocer's apostrophe): Apple's for sale; Open Tuesday's, Wednesday's, and Friday's.* The apostrophe is the curse of the English-speaking world, and one reader has reasonably suggested that in time it's bound to disappear. For now, never use the apostrophe in plural nouns unless the noun is possessive: *one dog, two dogs; one dog's bone, two dogs' bones.*

14. Saying *the reason being*, as in "I don't like slugs, the reason being that they make me choke." Much better is "I don't like slugs because they make me choke." Sometimes you hear a redundant *is*: "...the reason being is that they make me choke."

15. Saying "I seen" instead of "I saw." This is the error that provoked a strong desire in one reader to use physical violence. Using *seen* as the past tense of *see* is a glaring example of sub-standard English. Correct usage reflects society, of course, and if those who use *seen* as the past tense of *see* had political and economic power, it would be considered correct.

16. Saying *in regards to* as in "In regards to your grammar rules, I couldn't care less." It should be "In **regard** to..." with no *s*. One may say "As regards your grammar rules..." or "give my regards to Broadway," but one shouldn't say "in regards" to anything.

17. Mispronouncing *nuclear* as *noocyular*. This mispronunciation may be grating, but it is apparently not an impediment to achieving high elected office in the U.S.

18. Leaving out the *from* in *graduated* as in "She graduated high school with honours." Standard English requires *from:* "She graduated from high school." In fact, this usage is relatively recent. Before the early 19th century, only the passive was considered correct: "She was graduated from high school." The active voice emphasizes the accomplishment of the graduate. The use of *graduate* in this sense without *from* is common in some American dialects, but it should be avoided.

19. Leaving out the *of* in couple as in "I bought a couple packs of cigarettes." I am not sure where this originated, but it's probably most common among those who are too young to buy cigarettes.

20. Using *presently* to mean "at this time" as in "We are presently out of cash." Those who object strongly to this usage will be surprised to learn that it was common before the 17th century. At one time *presently* also meant "immediately." If you're inclined to be conservative regarding matters since the 17th century, use presently to mean only "in a short time."

21. Using *dilemma* as a synonym of *problem* or *difficult choice.* Technically, a dilemma is a choice between two options that are equally bad. Whether to drink the poison and die or refuse and be stoned to death is a dilemma. Whether to stick to my New Year's resolution or have another donut is a difficult choice.

22. Saying "there is" when it should be "there are": "There's four elephants coming down the street." Plural subjects require plural verbs, and in sentences that begin with *there is* or *there are*, the subject follows. *There are four elephants coming down the street* = *Four elephants are coming down the street.*

23. Using *loan* as a verb: "Can you loan me five dollars?" Actually, *loan* as a verb is a well established Americanism and is considered an error only in British usage and among English speakers who defer to the British. But even in non-British usage, *loan* doesn't sound right in figurative expressions: "Friends, Romans, countrymen, *loan* me you ears."

24. Using *since* to mean "because": "Since you can't come to the party, we're cancelling it." Using *since* with this meaning is not an error, but you have to be careful. Because *since* also has a temporal meaning—*I've been here since yesterday*—using it instead of *because* can cause ambiguity: "Since I've been in jail, I haven't read the book" can mean either that I haven't read the book while I've been in jail or that I haven't read it because I've been in jail.

25. Using *none* with a plural verb: "None of the voters are registered." It is an abiding myth that the indefinite pronoun *none* must take a singular verb. The myth's adherents insist that since etymologically *none* means "no one," it must be singular. But despite its origin, the sense of *none* is often "not any." In fact, depending on your intended meaning, *none* can be either singular or plural. "None (not one) of the voters is registered" or "None (not any) of the voters are registered" are equally acceptable. But add *almost,* and the plural is required: "Almost none of the voters are registered."

26. Using *went* instead of *gone* in the perfect tenses: "I should have went to the seminar." All verbs have three principle parts: present, past, and past participle (used with the auxiliary verbs *have* and *had*). For example, *walk (Today I walk), walked (Yesterday I walked), walked (I have often walked).* For regular verbs such as *walk*, the past and past participle are the same; for irregular verbs, they're different: *go, went, gone; swim, swam, swum; run, ran, run.* I went to the seminar. You should have gone to the seminar.

27. Using (cringe!) double negatives: *I could not hardly see what the teacher was writing on the blackboard.* Words such as *hardly, scarcely, barely* are negatives and can't be used with *not.*

28. Using a redundant *is: The reason is is that no one knows what redundant means.* I have never actually heard this, but I'm told that people are doing it. You know who you are. Stop it!

29. Using *tons* to mean "many": *There were tons of people at the party.* I'm not actually so disturbed by this sort of colloquialism. True, it's hard to imagine the Queen saying it. If you're interested in projecting a certain gravitas, avoid using *tons* in this sense.

30. Using dangling and misplaced modifiers*: Being the fitness coach, I think Colbart should lose some weight.* Whatever you think of Colbart's weight, you know very well that I'm not a fitness coach. The modifying phrase *Being the fitness coach* has to be followed by what it is supposed to modify, i.e., Colbart. *Being the fitness coach, Colbart should lose some weight.*

31. Using plural pronouns to refer to singular antecedents: *Sears stands behind their merchandise.* Sears might end in *s*, but it's still just one company, so **it** stands behind **its** merchandise.

32. Saying *between you and I.* This one keeps coming up. I've dealt with it in a couple of columns. It should be *between you and me* because *between* is a preposition (like *about, for, to, with,* etc.) and requires the object case pronoun. We need a critical mass of people to start saying *between you and me.* The downside is that some individuals will assume that we're the ones making the error.

33. Using *irregardless* for *regardless.* It's not quite true to say that there is no such word as "irregardless." It appears in dictionaries, but it's labelled non-standard. According to the *American Heritage Dictionary of the English Language, irregardless* is probably a blend of *irrespective* and *regardless.*

34. Using verbs (sometimes making them up) that end in –ize such as *finalize, optimize, strategize.* This is a tough one. However aesthetically unpleasing many of us find the sound of these verbs (and there's no accounting for taste), English produces them naturally. Few would object to *realize* or *moralize.* What we dislike is the overuse of such verbs in a context of jargon-laden prose: "A good CEO strategizes ways to incentivize staff to maximize their impactfulness customer relations-wise." Anyone who writes or speaks this way deserves to be vaporized.

35. Confusing *immigrate* and *emigrate.* One immigrates to a country and emigrates from one. From our point of view, an Italian *immigrates* to Canada and *emigrates* (God knows why) from Italy.

36. Using *momentarily* to mean "in a moment" as in "The plane will be landing momentarily." Although the word is frequently used with this meaning, most authorities insist that it should be used only to mean "for a moment."

37. Mixing up pronoun cases: "Don invited Dan and I over to play chess." Many who know that "Dan and I" is wrong in this sentence will say "Don invited Dan and myself over to play chess," which is just as bad. When the personal pronoun *I* is the object of a verb—in this case *invited*—it becomes *me.* This is a personal pet peeve, and I will surely mention it again.

38. Saying or writing "Like I said..." I suspect this is more common in American English than in Canadian English among teenagers. It should be "As I said..." *Like* can't introduce a clause. In standard English, one can't say, "You look like you've been waiting for a long time." Correct is "You look as if (or *as though*) you've been waiting for a long time."

39. Saying "I'm good" instead of "No thank you" or "I've had enough" when offered more of something. English has various levels of formality that are appropriate to various social relationships. To say "I'm good" when offered more wine at a formal dinner is certainly inappropriate. But using very formal language with a friend you're watching a movie with is also inappropriate. In some contexts, "I'm good" for "No thank you" is an acceptable colloquialism.

40. Using *lady* as a synonym for *woman* inappropriately: "The lady who spit on the sidewalk is disgusting." Reserve *lady* for occasions that require formality and courtesy "Ladies and Gentlemen, welcome to the Annual Grammar Police Convention." In informal situations, use *woman*. Never use *lady* as an adjective: *a lady doctor*. Using *lady* this way is considered offensive. Instead, say either "a *woman* doctor" or "a *female* doctor."

41. Writing (especially in a newspaper) "the accused killer." *The Associated Press Stylebook* condemns this usage. Because a person is innocent until proven guilty, the correct phrase is "the person accused of the killing."

42. Writing "lead" instead of "led" as the past tense of "lead." The rancher led (not lead) the horse to water. This is a common error, probably because "lead" (the metal) and "led" (past tense of *lead*) have the same pronunciation.

43. The redundant expression "enter in" as in "Enter in your email address." "Enter in" is not a phrasal verb. "Enter into" is a phrasal verb: "We entered into an agreement." One may say "Enter your email address in the box provided."

44. Using the past tense instead of an irregular past participle as in "I have never *drank* more than six beers at a party." It should be *drunk*, of course. Anybody who drinks six beers at a party can be forgiven for getting irregular participles wrong.

45. Using *who* where *whom* is required: "Who did you go to the party with?" Actually, this use of *who* is perfectly acceptable in informal English. "Whom did you go to the party with" is correct but sounds very stuffy. Immediately after the preposition, most native speakers will use *whom*: "With whom did you go to the party," but that also sounds stuffy. On the other hand, the title of Hemmingway's novel *For Whom the Bell Tolls* sounds fine, at least to me.

46. The use of "outside of" to denote a physical location: "He lives just outside of Ottawa." The inclusion of "of" is wrong here. Similarly, the book fell off (not *off of*) the table.

47. Tacking the suffix –wise onto words: "Grammarwise, the president has some serious problems." The suffix –wise meaning "in the direction of" or "in the manner of" occurs in certain words such as *clockwise.* The use of the suffix to mean "in regard to" is fairly recent and occurs mostly in jargon-filled business writing: "Profitwise, it has been a good year." Alternatives require more words: "When it comes to profit, it has been a good year." This is one case where more words are better. Unless you are one who *"managementwise, incentivizes* associates to *interface impactfully,"* avoid using –wise this way.

48. Using "nauseous" to mean "nauseated": "Marion feels nauseous whenever she sees her credit card bill." *Nauseous* means "nauseating." It's the credit card that is nauseous (or nauseating) because it makes Marion feel *nauseated.* If you feel nauseous, it means that you think you make others feel nauseated, which probably isn't the case.

49. Using "criteria" as a singular noun as in "We have just one criteria for a bartender: honesty." The singular is "criterion." Several words of Greek or Latin origin have their plurals in *a*: phenomenon—phenomena, medium—media, agendum—agenda. "Media" is slowly becoming accepted as a singular, and "agenda" is now completely accepted as a singular, but "criteria" is not.

50. Confusing "flaunt" and "flout" as in "The greedy CEO flaunted ethical considerations." A greedy CEO might flaunt (show off) the fancy clothes he has bought with his ill-gotten gains, but he flouted (contemptuously ignored) ethics to get them.

51. The expression "somewhat of a" as in "Colbart is somewhat of a clown." Colbart can be somewhat clownish or something of a clown, but not *somewhat of* an anything.

52. Speaking like a teenager. This is like okay if you like are a teenager?

53. Using "gotten" for "got" as in "Mort has gotten in trouble again." In American English "gotten" is preferred. British English prefers "got." Canadian English wavers between the two.

54. Using "good" as an adverb as in "I did good on the test." This usage immediately marks one as semi-literate. You do anything *well*, not good.

55. Mispronouncing "mischievous" as though it had four syllables: *mis-chie-vi-ous*. It has only three syllables, and the accent is on the first syllable.

56. Mispronouncing "espresso" as "expresso." As the owner of a high-end espresso machine and lover of all things Italian, I also find this mispronunciation extremely annoying.

57. Using apostrophes to make names plural: The Smith's live here. One Smith—two Smiths.

58. Saying "You know" all the time. I agree that all such verbal tics are annoying. I have run into people who are incapable of using an adjective without the tacking on the adverb "literally." Actually, I have a tendency to overuse "actually."

59. Saying "I could care less." Supposedly, this is an illogical scrambling of "I couldn't care less," meaning that I care so little that it would be impossible for me to care less. Having given it some thought, I'm no longer so sure. Said with the right intonation and visual cues (rolling the eyes, for example), "I could care less" may up the ante of sarcasm of the original. I can easily imagine a troublesome adolescent who has been told that he will flunk English saying, "Yeah, like I could care less." The meaning would be clear.

60. Forming a superlative adjective with both "most" and the suffix –est. On emerging from a tour of Westminster Abbey, my eight-year-old grandson exclaimed, "Westminster Abbey is the most boringest place on the planet." I admit that the error sounds stronger than "most boring" but only in the mouth of an eight-year-old.

61. The non-existent word "hisself" as in "He bought hisself a new car." Any word people say exists, of course, but some words are non-standard (*sub-standard* is too judgmental). Even an educated speaker of standard English can get tripped up. The following appeared recently in a highbrow magazine: "…any artist in any media, who is trying to manifest a work of any import, must transform his or herself into, a la Henry James, 'one upon whom nothing is wasted.'" It should be "him or herself."

62. The phrase "You may be rest assured" drives one reader crazy. Where does the "be" come from? I have no idea, but if I encountered this phrase very often, it would drive me crazy too.

63. Using "normalcy" for "normality." Actually, "normalcy" is perfectly acceptable, especially in American English.

64. Using the words "I mean" and "and stuff like that." We know that you mean what you say. We don't know what "stuff" you mean.

65. "I feel badly." This is a perennial pet peeve that I have mentioned many times. It may be such a widespread error that it's approaching acceptability. But I doubt that those who say "I feel badly" would ever think of saying "I feel wonderfully."

66. Confusing "everyday" and "every day" as in "She wears her every day clothes to church." Only the one-word version can be used as an adjective, so she wears *everyday* clothes. *Every day* means "each day." If you can't substitute "each day" and still make sense, use "everyday."

67. The insulting epithet "grammar Nazi" as in "Only a grammar Nazi could care about dangling modifiers." Okay, this is my pet peeve. "Nazi" is a much overused term of abuse. I prefer the term "grammar fussbudget."

READERS' QUESTIONS

I get many interesting questions about grammar. Here are some of them together with my answers:

Q: Which of these is correct: *cannot* or *can not*?

A: Both are acceptable, but *cannot* is more common. The two-word version can be used for emphasis: *No, you can **not** eat the salamander.*

Q: Which of these is correct: *in hospital* or *in the hospital*?

A: *In hospital* is British usage. Americans say *in the hospital.* Canadians generally follow British usage. Similarly, Brits (and Canadians) say *in* or *at* university. Americans say *in* or *at the university* or *in* or *at the college.* Note that *in hospital* refers only to a patient. Even in British usage, a doctor works in *the* hospital.

Q: Can the relative pronoun *that* refer to persons?

A: Yes. In restrictive clauses (clauses that identify the person we are talking about), one can use either *that* or *who: The politician that gets my vote has to be honest. The politician who gets my vote has to be honest.* Both are correct.

Q: Which of these is correct: *If I were you* or *If I was you?*

A: Use *were* in *if* clauses that are contrary to fact: *If I were rich, I would be living in southern France.* Clearly *If I were you* is contrary to fact. In *if* clauses that are not necessarily contrary to fact, use *was* (except for plural, of course): *If she was at the party, I didn't see her.*

Q: Is it correct to say, "Soccer is so fun"?

A: *Soccer is so fun* is incorrect in formal English, although this use of the word *fun* is common in spoken English. *Fun* is a noun, and in the sentence *Soccer is so fun,* it is being used as an adjective like *amusing* or *enjoyable.* In formal English one would have to say *Soccer is so amusing* or *Soccer is so enjoyable.*

Q: Is it correct to say, "I'll try and do it by tomorrow"?

A: No. One should say, "I'll try to do it by tomorrow."

Q: Doesn't the expression *aren't I* violate subject/verb agreement since *I* is singular and *are* is plural?

A: Yes. There is no accepted contraction for *I am not* in formal English. By analogy with *isn't* and *aren't,* you would think we would have *am't,* but we don't. The use of the contraction *aren't* (for *are not*) with *I* is widespread in spoken English, probably because *am I not* sounds a bit stilted.

Q: Why is the Biblical verse "The wages of sin is death"? Shouldn't it be "The wages of sin <u>are</u> death"?

A: *Wages,* meaning "a fitting return; a recompense," can be used with either a plural or a singular verb. It appears as "The wages of sin is death" in most translations of the Bible. *The Weymouth New Testament Online Bible (WEY)* has "The wages of sin are death." (Romans 6:23) This one I had to research.

Q: Is *woken up* correct as in "I had woken up before dinner"? Shouldn't it be *awakened?*

A: *Woken* is grammatically correct. One can say either *awakened* or *woken up.* The principal parts of the verb *wake* are *wake, woke* or *waked, woken.* Both verbs can be used as follows. *I woke up/I* *awakened* (never *I awakened up); I woke him up/I awakened him. Awaken* is more common figuratively: *Grammar awakens a sense of dread in me.*

Q: Is *orient,* as in "He stood for a moment to orient himself," correct, or should it be *orientate?*

A: Most style manuals object to *orientate.* Supposedly it is a back formation; that is, the original verb is *orient,* but another verb—*orientate*—was formed from the noun *orientation. Orientate* is standard in British usage, but *orient* is preferred in North American usage.

Q: What is the correct verb in this sentence? "Your patience and support (are/is) appreciated."

A: Two nouns joined by *and* make a plural subject, so the correct verb is *are.*

Q: What part of speech is the verb *wait* in the sentence "There is nothing I can do but wait"?

A: In your sentence, *wait* is what some grammarians call a *bare infinitive.* The infinitive in English normally includes *to*: *to wait.* But after certain verbs (**will, shall, would, could, can, may, might, must, should** and **needn't**) the infinitive doesn't have the *to.* We don't say "I can *to wait."* In the sentence "There is nothing I can do but wait," both *do* and *wait* are bare infinitives after the verb *can.*

Q: Should the verb in this sentence be singular or plural: "The police (warn/warns) the public to stay away from the area"?

A: The noun *police,* like *people,* is always plural. The correct verb is *warn.*

Q: I often hear the expression "I could care less." Shouldn't it be "I couldn't care less."

A: Originally the expression is "I couldn't care less," meaning that caring less is impossible because I don't care at all. "I could care less" implies I care at least a little and is probably just a careless garbling of the original.

Q: Should it be *none is* or *none are?*

A: *None* can be either singular or plural. The notion that it is only singular is a grammatical myth. *None of the students (is* or *are) here.* Both are acceptable. When *none* clearly refers to a singular noun, the verb must be singular: *None of the cake has been eaten.*

Q: What is the difference between *which* and *that*.

A: Both *which* and *that* can be used to introduce essential relative clauses. *The dog that* (or *which) ate my boots is dead.* The clause "that ate my boots" is essential because it identifies the dog I am talking about. Only *which* can introduce non-essential clauses: *The Smiths' dog, which ate my boots, is dead.* The clause "which ate my boots" is non-essential because I have already identified the dog. Non-essential clauses are always set off by commas; essential clauses never are. Style guides for journalists (Associated Press, Canadian Press) tell writers to use only *that* for essential clauses.

For essential relative clauses that refer to persons, use *who* or *that: The man who* (or *that) ate my boots is in jail.* For non-essential clauses that refer to persons, use only *who: Mr. Jones, who ate my boots, is in jail.*

Q: Which is correct? Please get the laundry basket from (Dad and my) (Dad's and my) bedroom.

A: "Dad's and my bedroom," meaning "the bedroom belonging to Dad and me" is correct. Note that if two nouns are used, only the second noun is possessive: *Mom and Dad's bedroom.* This is true, though, only for joint possession. For separately owned items, both nouns are possessive: *Mom's and Dad's signatures.*

Q: Would you please comment on the use of the term "one off"?

A: As an adjective *one-off* (it's hyphenated) means "happening, done, or made only once." As a noun it means "something that is not repeated or reproduced." The word is chiefly British.

Q: I constantly hear people say "I've got" in their sentences and I think that is incorrect. Shouldn't it be "I have"?

A: "I've got" for "I have" is standard usage in Canadian English. The past participle "gotten" is also used to some extent with interesting distinctions. According to the *Columbia Guide to Standard American English,* "I've got some money" means 'I have some money'; *I've gotten some money* means 'I've obtained some money.'"

Q: If a group of corporate vice-presidents issues an annual report and included is a group message from all six, what should the title of that message be: Vice-Presidents' Message or Vice-Presidents Message?

A: Vice-Presidents' message.

Q: Many people use the phrase "gone missing" or "went missing" when talking about a missing person's case. Is it grammatically correct or just used so often it sounds right?

A: *To go missing* meaning "to disappear" is an acceptable idiom, but it is more common in British than in Canadian usage.

Q: A friend of mine uses words *quite unique* or *very unique* all the time to describe things or situations he likes. Is it correct?

A: *Unique* is an absolute adjective meaning "one of a kind" and can't be modified. Something can't be quite (or very) unique or more unique than something else. *The cabinets Harold designed are unique.*

Q: Are commas not supposed to come after an introductory phrase at the start of a sentence? I was always taught that if something is taken from elsewhere in the sentence and put at the beginning, then a comma is required: "We plan to visit Spain this year" becomes "This year, we plan to visit Spain." Isn't this correct? And is there ever a time when a comma isn't required, or am I just reading a lot of incorrect writing?

A: The comma can be eliminated after short introductory phrases such as "this year" but not after long introductory phrases (more than four words) – *In the spring of 1971, we moved to*

Canada. Participial and infinitive phrases used as modifiers must be set off by a comma: *Walking down the street, we spotted the dog.* (Participial modifier) *To pass this course, you have to attend every class.* (Infinitive modifier)

Q: Is it correct to say "I have less than five dollars," or should one say "I have fewer than five dollars"?

A: Although it is true that we use "fewer" for anything we can count— fewer cookies—in the case of money, time or distance, we use less: *less than five dollars, less than five hours, less than five miles.* But if we're counting individual bills, we use "fewer": *I have fewer Australian dollars than I used to.*

GRAMMAR RESOLUTIONS

Here are my grammar and language resolutions. Pick the ones that apply to you.

1. I resolve to stop using the reflexive pronoun *myself* in contexts that require the object pronoun *me.* (The boss invited my wife and myself (ugh!) to dinner.)

2. I resolve to stop using the subject pronoun *I* in contexts that require the object pronoun *me.* (The boss invited my wife and I (ugh!) to dinner.)

3. I resolve to stop using *dilemma* as a synonym for *a difficult problem.*

4. I resolve to use *dilemma* as a synonym for *a difficult problem* and not worry about it.

5. I resolve to write at least one paragraph of postmodern literary criticism that even my grandmother could understand.

6. I resolve never to say "between you and I" instead of "between you and me" even though "between you and I" was apparently not considered an error in Shakespeare's day.

7. I resolve to write a memo without any jargon or buzzwords just to see what happens.

8. I resolve never to use *less* instead of *fewer* with nouns that can be counted. (Eat fewer (not less) cookies.)

9. I resolve never to confuse *it's* and *its.* (It's a shame the dog broke its tail.)

10. I resolve never to use five words for one. (due to the fact that = because.)

11. I resolve to stop using the wordy phrase "when all is said and done."

12. I resolve to stop using the comma as a decoration.

13. I resolve to always ask what *incentivize* means and act surprised when I'm told.

14. I resolve to split infinitives and end sentences with prepositions whenever it seems appropriate.

15. I resolve to stop writing the non-existent word *alot. (*A lot of students do this.)

16. I resolve to confine obscure abbreviations to text messaging.

17. I resolve never to insult a reader's intelligence by putting a happy face at the end of a joke.

18. I resolve to avoid using trendy buzzwords (buzz phrases, not so much).

19. I resolve to break off all relations with anybody who says "the exact same" anything.

20. I resolve to say "at the end of the day" only at sundown.

21. I resolve to stop wasting my employees' time with vague, wordy memos.

22. I resolve to stop using "literally" to mean "figuratively": *The cat literally ate us out of our house and home.* No, it didn't.

23. I resolve to stop getting worked up over the "15 items or less" sign at the supermarket.

24. I resolve to recognize that the way teenagers talk does presage the end of civilization.

25. I resolve to stop saying "at this point in time."

26. I resolve eliminate "the fact that" from my writing: despite the fact that = although.

27. I resolve to learn once and for all what a comma splice is.

28. I resolve to learn the difference between "lay" and "lie" or avoid using them: "The cat is not standing up on the couch."

29. I resolve to start using the object pronoun "me" when it's appropriate even if I think it sounds wrong: "The Grand Jury indicted the vice-president and me (not *I*) for fraud."

30. I resolve to give up the myth that sentences can't begin with "and" or "but." But I will avoid beginning sentences with "however."

31. I resolve to use "impact" as a synonym for "affect" only in truly dramatic contexts: "Itchy eyebrows affect (not *impact*) my concentration."

32. I resolve to revive and use at least one solid, ordinary word in place of an elegant alternative: "Uncle Charlie will be in prison (not *a correctional facility*) this New Year's Eve."

33. I resolve to stop saying "I feel badly" and feel inwardly superior to those who do: "I feel bad (not *badly*) about Uncle Charlie."

34. I resolve to stop making plurals with apostrophes: *Banana's (ugh!) for sale*, and learn once and for all how to use apostrophes or make a large contribution to The Apostrophe Protection Society (**http://www.apostrophe.fsnet.co.uk/**).

35. I resolve to strive for conciseness and clarity in writing: "If (not *In the event that*) you can't (not *you do not find yourself in a position to*) stop (not *cease and desist*) drinking (not *imbibing alcoholic beverages*), I will file for (not *commence legal proceedings toward*) divorce (not *a termination of our marriage*).

36. I resolve to pronounce "et cetera" correctly.

37. I resolve to stop using the expression "I have issues with" and just say what I mean: "I loathe (not *have issues with*) your mother's cat."

38. I resolve to break off all relations with anyone, even one of my children, who consistently uses "awesome" to describe things that aren't actually awesome.

39. I resolve that when somebody thanks me, I will say, "You're welcome," not "Thank *you!*"

40. I resolve to use "eh?" as a tag question only when speaking to my cousins down South: "So, your money's not worth so much anymore, eh?"

41. I resolve (unless I move to the UK) to put periods inside final quotation marks.

42. I resolve to avoid potentially offensive misplaced and dangling modifiers: "Being no longer of any use to anybody, Grandma decided to throw out my late Uncle Stanley's pipe collection."

43. I resolve to stop using the hyphenated "thank-you" except as an adjective: "Thank you (not *Thank-you*) for the thank-you note."

44. I resolve to use happy faces only in emails I send to small children.

45. I resolve to place the modifier *only* directly in front of the words it's supposed to modify: I read **only** three pages.

46. I resolve not to worry about placement of the modifier *only* when the meaning is clear: I **only** read three pages.

47. I resolve to send all my pet peeves about others' grammatical errors to *How to Avoid Grammar Gaffes Once and for All.*

48. I resolve to enjoy and celebrate the ever changing nature and wild diversity of style and register that are inherent in a living language.

QUIZZES

How to Avoid Grammar Gaffes Once and for All **ends with a major review quiz. Test your knowledge and get your score at the end of this chapter.**

Choose the correct word:

1. Losing $5,000 at the casino (affected/effected) my mood.
2. We felt (bad/badly) about your accident.
3. Last night we stayed at my (aunt and uncle's/aunt's and uncle's) place.
4. Just between you and (I/me), I think grammar is overrated.
5. If you have any questions, give Mel or (I/myself/me) a call.
6. Give the puppy to (whoever/whomever) can provide a good home.
7. Unless you're a cat, just (laying/lying) around all day gets boring.
8. Because I read *How to Avoid Grammar Gaffes Once and for All*, I make (less/fewer) mistakes than I used to make.

Answers: **1.** affected **2.** bad **3.** aunt and uncle's **4.** me **5.** me **6.** whoever **7.** lying **8.** fewer

Translate the following wordy sentences into normal English:

1. There were a lot of cars that were damaged by vandals last night.

2. High-quality footwear designed specifically for winter weather conditions greatly enhances the ambulatory navigation of icy surfaces.

Answers: 1. Vandals damaged many cars last night. **2.** Good winter boots make walking on ice easier.

Choose the correct word:

1. Piranhas never feel (bad/badly) about their behaviour.

2. (Our's/Ours) is the only dog on the block that has never chased a cat.

3. The (Jones's/Joneses') cat went missing.

4. The neighbours like the dog, but they loath (him/his) howling at the moon.

5. Give my secretary or (I/myself/me) a call if you have any questions.

6. Give the job to (whoever/whomever) you think is the best candidate.

7. It is a great pleasure for the Prime Minister and (I/myself/me) to welcome you this evening.

8. If she (was/were) at the party, no one saw her.

9. If I (were/was) in better shape, I would take up mountain climbing.

10. We (couldn't/could) hardly believe how hard he worked.

11. If you (would have/had) told me about the party sooner, I would have come.

12. (Its/It's) a good thing you remembered to feed the cat.

13. Just between you and (I/me), Shakespeare isn't a very good guide to modern usage.

14. Neither the secretaries nor the office manager (plan/plans) to attend the meeting.

15. Neither Susan nor I (is/am) planning to attend.

16. The original document, along with all subsequent copies, (was/were) lost.

17. McDonald's has added many new items to (its/their) menu.

18. Things didn't quite turn out (like/as) she had predicted.

19. How will being sued and losing your job (affect/effect) you financially?

20. We bought the (friskiest/friskier) of the two puppies.

21. Your uncle has (lain/laid) on the sofa all day.

22. No one who has experienced an Edmonton (Winter/winter) fears global warming.

23. We should (of/have) known the cat would destroy the carpet.

24. Dad went to buy Mom some good walking shoes, but he couldn't find the (womens'/women's) department.

Answers: **1.** bad **2.** Ours **3.** Joneses' **4.** his **5.** me **6.** whoever **7.** me **8.** was **9.** were **10.** could **11.** had **12.** It's **13.** me **14.** plans **15.** am **16.** was **17.** its **18.** as **19.** affect **20.** friskier **21.** lain **22.** winter **23.** have **24.** women's

Choose the correctly punctuated sentence:

1. **a.** The game, which intrigues me most, is chess.
   b. The game that intrigues me most is chess.
2. **a.** My sister Kate, who lives in Kansas, is a great cook.
   b. My sister Kate who lives in Kansas is a great cook.
3. **a.** Because failure frightens him he never tries.
   b. Because failure frightens him, he never tries.
4. **a.** Will you please close the door when you leave
   b. Will you please close the door when you leave.
5. **a.** "What," she asked, "does that have to do with it"?
   b. "What," she asked, "does that have to do with it?"
6. **a.** I never eat frogs because they make me sick.
   b. I never eat frogs, because they make me sick.
7. **a.** Have you ever read *War and Peace*?
   b. Have you ever read "War and Peace"?

Answers: **1. b** **2. a** **3. b** **4. b** (A polite request has the form of a question, but it's punctuated with a period.) **5. b** **6. a** **7. a**

Choose the correct word:

1. Colbart tried hard to (affect/effect) an air of sophistication.
2. Jadwiga (lead/led) the Scout troop into the swamp.
3. Abigail soon became bored (of/with) watching the guinea pig eat.
4. Zilpah left a dead mouse (laying/lying) on the pillow.
5. Nobody wanted to hear the (grisly/grizzly) details of Bert's night out.
6. Cecil was not (adverse/averse) to flattery.
7. (We/Us) grammar gurus don't get invited to (alot/a lot) of parties.
8. The mugger was a (friendly-looking/friendly looking) gentleman in his mid-fifties.
9. Francine and (I/me/myself) are planning a party to celebrate Grandpa's release from prison.
10. Even the most (carefully-planned/carefully planned) strategy can fail.

Answers: **1.** affect **2.** led **3.** with **4.** lying **5.** grisly **6.** averse **7.** We, a lot **8.** friendly-looking **9.** I **10.** carefully planned

Choose the correctly punctuated sentence:

1. **a.** Gloria loves to dance but almost never goes dancing.
b. Gloria loves to dance, but almost never goes dancing.

2. **a.** Mort enjoys a good movie, but he almost never has time to watch one.
b. Mort enjoys a good movie but he almost never has time to watch one.

3. **a.** We have to keep the door to the living room closed; otherwise, the cat will destroy the furniture.
b. We have to keep the door to the living room closed, otherwise, the cat will destroy the furniture.

4. **a.** The economist said, "To err is human; to get paid for it is divine".
b. The economist said, "To err is human; to get paid for it is divine."

5. **a.** Was it Woody Allen who said, "Eighty percent of success is showing up"?
   b. Was it Woody Allen who said, "Eighty percent of success is showing up?"
6. **a.** Ask me if you have any questions.
   b. Ask me, if you have any questions.
7. **a.** Would you please close the door.
   b. Would you please close the door?

Answers: 1. a 2. a 3. a 4. b 5. a 6. a 7. a

Revise the following sentences to eliminate misplaced and dangling modifiers (words or phrases that are out of place and give the sentences unintended meanings).

1. When defrosted, cut the steaks into strips.
2. Before going to bed, Jasmine always drinks a hot cup of chocolate.
3. Looking back, the cat was stalking us.
4. Marge found a scarf in the drawer that doesn't belong to her.
5. I only got three answers right.

Possible revisions:

1. When the steaks are defrosted, cut them into strips.
2. Before going to bed, Jasmine always has a cup of hot chocolate.
3. Looking back, we saw the cat stalking us.
4. Marge found a scarf that doesn't belong to her in the drawer.
5. I got only three answers right.

Choose the correct word:

1. Of the two cats, Isabella is by far the (smarter/smartest).
2. Wayne had to admit that Cheryl's humus was (tastier/more tasty) than his.
3. The policeman (that/who) gave Merrill and Linda a ticket has been fired.

4. Chrystia was taken (aback/back) by Ivan's objection to her score keeping.

5. Give the book to (whoever/whomever) wants it.

Answers: 1. smarter **2.** tastier **3.** either (It is a widely believed myth that the pronoun "that" can never refer to persons. If the person is anonymous, one can use either "that" or "who.") **4.** aback **5.** whoever

Spot the errors in the following sentences:

1. Ursula used to walk Theo everyday.
2. Saul and Sara could of danced all night.
3. Bluma's inability to tell blood from cinnamon made her an unlikely candidate for medical school.
4. Saskatchewan has better restaurants than any province in Canada.
5. If you fear that what you have to say is stupid, use alot of big words.

Answers: 1. Ursula used to walk Theo **every day. 2.** Saul and Sara could **have** danced all night. **3.** no comma. **4.** Saskatchewan has better restaurants than any **other** province in Canada. **5.** …use **a lot** of big words.

Choose the correctly punctuated sentence:

1. **a.** Anna bought David a book called *How Eating Apricots Can Raise your IQ and Make You Sexually Irresistible.*

   b. Anna bought David a book called "How Eating Apricots Can Raise your IQ and Make You Sexually Irresistible."

2. **a.** The O'Briens live up the street.

   b. The O'Brien's live up the street.

3. **a.** John-Paul claims he isn't superstitious; however, he won't shake hands over a threshold.

   b. John-Paul claims he isn't superstitious, however, he won't shake hands over a threshold.

4. **a.** "Why," Abigail asked, "do you never know the answer to anything"?

b. "Why," Abigail asked, "do you never know the answer to anything?"

5. **a.** Colbart's recipe for success includes always laughing at the jokes of important people, checking his socks for holes, and never slurping soup.

b. Colbart's recipe for success includes: always laughing at the jokes of important people, checking his socks for holes, and never slurping soup.

Answers: 1. a 2. a 3. a 4. b 5. a

Revise the following sentences to correct misplaced and dangling modifiers:

1. Walking to the car, my arm was broken in a nasty fall.
2. Ada found a scarf in the drawer that doesn't belong to her.
3. Take a look at the policy that is enclosed with your wife.
4. Marg greeted the mailman wearing only her pyjamas.
5. We're looking for someone to house sit and take care of our dog who doesn't drink.

Answers: **1.** Walking to the car, I broke my arm in a nasty fall. **2.** Ada found a scarf that doesn't belong to her in the drawer. **3.** Take a look at the enclosed policy with your wife. **4.** Wearing only her pyjamas, Marg greeted the mailman. **5.** We're looking for someone who doesn't drink to house sit and take care of our dog.

What your score means:

0–5

The importance of grammar is greatly exaggerated.

6–10

You are not an elitist snob.

10–15

You have to make an effort to tone it down when you go bowling.

15–20

Most people think you're the one making mistakes.

This is, alas, the end of How to Avoid Grammar Gaffes Once and for All. I have enjoyed writing it. I have especially enjoyed hearing from thoughtful readers. Believe it or not, I haven't always known the answers to your questions off the top, and I have learned much from researching them. Your comments and insights have led me to abandon some grammatical dogmas. For example, I no longer studiously avoid using hopefully to mean "it is to be hoped," and, hopefully, neither will you.

Alan Rutkowski

INDEX

A

E

I

J

L

O

P

S

www.ingramcontent.com/pod-product-compliance
Lightning Source LLC
Chambersburg PA
CBHW051951090426
42741CB00008B/1353

* 9 7 8 0 9 6 9 3 6 5 8 8 4 *